Contemporary Political Philosophy

Contemporary Political Philosophy

RADICAL STUDIES

EDITED BY
KEITH GRAHAM
Lecturer in Philosophy
University of Bristol

CAMBRIDGE UNIVERSITY PRESS
Cambridge
London New York New Rochelle
Melbourne Sydney

Published by the Press Syndicate of the University of Cambridge
The Pitt Building, Trumpington Street, Cambridge CB2 1RP
32 East 57th Street, New York, NY 10022, USA
296 Beaconsfield Parade, Middle Park, Melbourne 3206, Australia

First published 1982

Printed in Great Britain at the Pitman Press, Bath

Library of Congress catalogue card number: 81–21599

British Library Cataloguing in Publication Data

Contemporary political philosophy
1. Political science—Addresses, essays,
lectures
I. Graham, Keith
320′.01 JA41

ISBN 0 521 24551 6 hard covers
ISBN 0 521 28783 9 paperback

Contents

Contributors

TED BENTON, *Lecturer in the Sociology Department at the University of Essex*

JOHN HARRIS, *Lecturer in Philosophy in the Department of Education, University of Manchester*

RUSSELL KEAT, *Lecturer in Philosophy at the University of Lancaster*

RICHARD NORMAN, *Lecturer in Philosophy at the University of Kent*

KEITH GRAHAM, *Lecturer in Philosophy at the University of Bristol*

ANTHONY SKILLEN, *Lecturer in Philosophy at the University of Kent*

Introduction

1

Political philosophy is in an exciting phase. In a relatively short space of time the intellectual climate of the discipline has been transformed. It is only a few years since political philosophy was thought to have been killed by positivism and the later development of linguistic philosophy, so that the most which could usefully be done in the area was the clarification of political terms. In fact, however, the traditional (often normative) questions raised in political thinking never disappeared and are now once again firmly at the centre of debate.

Two important factors can be discerned in the process which has led to this regeneration of the discipline. On the one hand, there is the reappearance of very substantial original texts in the subject, well-known works like Robert Nozick's *Anarchy, state and Utopia* and John Rawls's *A theory of justice*, which have themselves generated a very considerable secondary literature in political philosophy and adjacent areas. This represents a return to an earlier style of work. But the second factor represents a new departure in the Anglophone tradition. In the last twenty years or so Marxism has come to be taken seriously as an intellectual position rather than as merely a partisan political stance. Marx's own writings have received close and scholarly scrutiny, the work of a number of continental Marxists has become influential, and here too a new volume of literature has come into being.

The interconnected essays in this collection make a significant contribution in the context I have outlined. They could all be described as radical, in more than one sense. They are radical in that, like all good philosophy, they question and challenge the received wisdom. More importantly, the essays are radical in focusing on the fundamental principles and arguments underlying particular political postures. They might for those reasons be categorised as radical in the political sense, but appearance may be misleading here. There are in fact wide political differences between the contributors, and it is the received wisdom of the left as much as that of the supporters of the *status quo* which is subjected to scrutiny in the pages which follow.

2

When people espouse and argue about political ideals (and the number of such ideals seriously embraced is remarkably small), they do so against a background of assumptions about what people themselves are like, and they must relate those ideals to some conception of what is possible and appropriate by way of social organisation and behaviour. The three parts of this book deal respectively with these three areas of theory: notions of human nature as they affect political possibilities; the articulation and development of particular political ideals; and the nature and limits of human organisation.

Human beings have interests and needs. This much is a platitude (though one with political implications), but little else can be said so uncontroversially. In particular it is a matter of dispute whether it makes sense to ascribe to people interests which they themselves do not recognise. The issue is of some importance, since it is in this connection that the Rousseauian idea is mooted that people must be forced to be free. In the first paper in part I, Benton discusses the matter in the context of recent work by Lukes and Connolly. He argues that the concept of interests is irreducibly both cognitive and normative, a fact carrying implications for the arguments of both Marxist and behaviourist political scientists, as he tries to show.

It is clear that certain needs and interests can be ascribed to all people in virtue of their common humanity, and that this places constraints on ways in which they may legitimately be treated. But there is a problem about the exact scope of this notion of a person as it affects issues of political liberty. Are children to count as persons? Harris argues that the grounds usually given to justify paternalism towards children apply equally to many adults. He attempts to give an acceptable account of personhood, connecting it with the idea of a creature which sees value in its own life, and suggests that we may simply have to change our views about the political status of some (though not young) children, rather than supposing that there is an as-yet-undiscovered rationale for our present attitudes.

In part II the network of ideals on which contemporary political argument is based is confronted directly. In discussion of political ideals, many Marxists are scathing about bourgeois talk of various human rights; in return, many liberals believe it is no accident that societies which supposedly organise themselves on Marxist principles are totalitarian in character – a claim recently made by Kolakowski. Keat explores this question via a consideration of Marx's discussion of rights in 'On the Jewish question'. He examines the division of life into private and political spheres, considers how far the two can merge into each other and stresses the importance for socialists of developing a conception of community which is not simply a return to ideas of the pre-individualist past. Along the way he relates his argument to Rawls's theory of justice.

Claims for equality are often based on data of the sort discussed in part I, but equality is not a universally shared aspiration in our political culture. Liberty, on the other hand, probably is, and it is sometimes argued by conservatives that the two ideals are incompatible, that attempts to secure equality must diminish liberty. Norman argues that, on the contrary, the two are interdependent. He defends a conception of positive freedom, emphasising the importance of material and other prerequisites, and suggests that an egalitarian programme must secure equal liberty. Finally, the claim that equality must result in lower overall liberty is shown to be implausible.

In part III issues to do with acceptable forms of political organisation, and behaviour within them, are raised.

The problem of the grounds for obedience to state authority is as old as political philosophy itself. Graham examines the recent debate over Wolff's claim that no room is left for such obedience when one takes seriously one's role as a moral agent. He resists the anarchist conclusion to that effect, and considers different possible forms of democratic organisation. He concludes that existing forms fall short of what is required, and sketches a more acceptable model.

Freedom of speech is an issue which crops up in legislative matters both in America and in Britain. Skillen offers a revised libertarian position, pointing out the weakness in many current arguments for curtailment of speech and stressing the connection between the freedom to express beliefs and the sense of one's own identity. He provides an account of the constituents of full freedom of speech, paying attention to the role of the media and the audience, and outlines the nature of sensible restrictions on this freedom.

3

It is easy enough to discuss the perennial issues of political philosophy, but it is not always easy to do so with the high regard for clarity of argument and expression aspired to by the contributors, or with a feeling for their bearing on concrete questions of political practice. In the pages which follow there is considerable response to the contemporary literature of the subject, but always in the interest of developing some positive position. The collection covers a wide range of questions, with comments on immediate issues, such as Eurocommunism and civil rights movements, as well as broader ones like equality of opportunity and the rejection of parliamentary democracy.

It is hoped that the collection will provide material for seminars, as well as being of interest to other academics.

PART I

Human Nature

1 *Realism, power and objective interests*

TED BENTON

1 *Introduction*

Recent debates surrounding the work of Steven Lukes, W. E. Connolly[1] and others on the concepts of 'power' and 'interests' show an interesting convergence with certain persistent problems of Marxist theory and practice. Both traditions have recently posed in an acute way questions about the possibility and/or desirability of 'objective', 'value-neutral' or 'scientific' political theory and, connectedly, about the necessity of presuppositions of a moral or political nature in the definitions of the key concepts of political analysis.

These questions are in turn connected, for both traditions, with questions as to the coherence or desirability in political analysis of characterisations of political relationships which depart from, or even contradict, characterisations adopted by participant actors themselves. It seems that, on the one hand, cognitively and politically significant features of prevailing social and political systems are arbitrarily shut off from political analysis if participant actors' characterisations are regarded as ultimate. On the other hand, attempts to replace participants' characterisations seem necessarily to involve a degree of arbitrariness, value-bias and, consequently, contestability which threatens to undermine the claim to objectivity or scientificity on the part of the political analyst.

But the dilemma has implications which go far beyond this apparent threat to the professional self-esteem of the political analyst. In so far as political analyses are intended to be, or are in fact, used as resources in the formation and justification of public policy, then so far do the conceptual decisions of political analysts play a practical part in the political process itself. If we

[1] See, in particular, Lukes 1976 and Connolly 1974.

consider, as an example, the concept of 'interests', it is clear that any ascription, in political analysis, of interests to actors which are in conflict with the self-ascriptions of interests which those actors deploy may license the advocacy of public policies inimical to the express preferences of those actors as, nevertheless, in their 'real interests'. Steven Lukes, for example, mentions, and tries to guard against, the use of the conception of real interests which he advocates as a 'paternalist licence for tyranny'.

In what follows I shall attempt, first of all, to clarify what is at stake in this nexus of problems and questions. Second, I shall attempt to show that Lukes, Connolly *et al.* are insufficiently radical in their critiques of empiricist and behaviourist political science. In continuing to share important assumptions with the latter, they unnecessarily weaken their case against it. In particular, I shall argue that it is possible to construct a concept of power which is available for empirical research, which enables analysis of those aspects of social and political systems foreclosed by empiricist and behaviourist political science, and yet which is not susceptible to the charge of moral or political bias. This argument is intended to sustain the idea of an objective approach to scientific analysis (though not a politically neutral one). Next, I shall attempt to argue that those who suppose that *all* the concepts of political discourse can be deprived of their evaluative presuppositions and made available for objective political analysis are also mistaken. The concept of interests is, I shall argue, a concept which is indispensably both cognitive and evaluative. Both Marxist and behaviourist political scientists who have attempted to use it in ostensibly 'objective' and 'scientific' analyses have either imposed their own evaluative presuppositions on the situations they have analysed, or they have employed the terminology of interests to mark some quite distinct concept.

My intention here is to encourage recognition of two quite distinct, though related, types of discourse, which are in turn interwoven with two distinct types of social practice: first, scientific discourse, governed by rules, procedures and values such that concept-formation and correction is subordinated to the priority of achieving objective knowledge of the relationships, processes and transformations of its objects; second, the discourses of tactical and strategic debate, contestation, legitimation and persuasion. Among the costs of conflating the first type of discourse into the second is that practical debate in and about politics is thereby deprived of a source of clarification, and a major resource for its advancement, and degenerates towards the mere articulation of pipe-dreams. Among the costs of the reverse conflation is the pseudo-scientific legitimation of tyranny. Finally, I propose to argue that recognition of this distinction is among the prerequisites for any democratic socialist strategy.

2 *What are the issues?*

Radical, but non-Marxist, critics of the predominantly empiricist, behaviourist and 'pluralist' orthodoxy in political science, notably Steven Lukes and W. E. Connolly, have centred their critique upon the identification of what they see as a significant aspect of power relations which is excluded from empirical analysis by the epistemological, ontological and methodological assumptions of the dominant tradition. The aspect of power relations to which they draw attention is the complex of processes whereby consent, often active consent, on the part of an underlying population, to specific exercises of power over them is secured. If it is an exercise of power when A secures the compliance of B with A's wishes, even against the wishes of B, then surely it is also an exercise of power when A secures the compliance of B by modifying B's very *wishes* in accordance with his (A's) objectives.

Of course, on this very simple model, the relationship could be assimilated to one of manipulation, whereby A offers inducements, or misleading characterisations of the likely consequences of the fulfilment of B's wishes which are calculated to bring about a change of mind. Such manipulative techniques *are* accessible to empiricist and behaviourist analysis, in so far as they are constituted by detectable actions and decisions of assignable individual actors. More serious from the point of view of the dominant tradition in political science is the claim that more or less persistent forms of social relationships, and the social practices they sustain, tend to structure and constrain the pattern of wants and aspirations which social actors are able to recognise and articulate. If it is possible for certain actors or groups of actors, in virtue of their social position, to sustain or modify these social forms and practices in such a way that the resulting pattern of wants in actors subject to them favours the non-conflictual realisation of their own wants and aspirations, then this is a situation uninvestigable as a power relationship by the dominant research tradition. The empiricism of the latter requires the observability of exercises of power, in the form of decisions and actions of specifiable actors, which settle conflicts of preferences or wants between contending actors or groups of actors. In the postulated type of case, power is exercised to ensure that conflicts over the mutually exclusive satisfaction of wants never arise. Moreover, the social processes whereby wants are formed typically consist in the day-to-day performance of taken-for-granted activities within a framework of broadly unquestioned social forms. The identification of specific acts of assignable actors as causally responsible for the formation of this or that want would be methodologically out of the question. Though it is generally the case that radical critics of the dominant tradition of power research tend to think that there are, as a matter of fact, such forms of power relationship which do remain uninvestigated by that tradition, this is not necessary to their critique. All that is required is the conceptual possibility of such relationships.

Suppose that powerful groups and individuals are able to affect the processes whereby the pattern of felt and articulated wants of the underlying population is formed in such a way that these wants are generally satisfiable within the framework of the prevailing social, economic and political institutions, and in such a way as not to obstruct the want-satisfaction of the power-holders. In such a society, research which is conceptually and methodologically restricted to the analysis of conflicts over the satisfaction of articulated wants within that institutional framework will contribute to the legitimation of such a situation in at least two respects. First, it will fail to register unarticulated wants, potential aspirations, possible preferences, which *might* have been formed, articulated, etc., were it not for the persistent relationships and practices which socially shape wants and preferences in that society. Secondly, in taking as 'given' the wants, preferences, etc. which *are* articulated, the power relations implicated in the processes of social production of those 'given' wants are rendered 'invisible'.

In so far as it is possible to argue that the pattern of articulated wants which is both produced and satisfied by the prevailing social order is unrepresentative of the true needs or interests of the mass of the population, and that the satisfaction of those needs or realisation of those interests is incompatible with the prevailing institutional framework, then so far is it possible to identify a conservative bias in research which is unable to detect the relevant relationships and processes. Again, though, it has to be stressed that the dominant empiricist and behaviourist perspective for power research by no means guarantees the results of its own application. The idea of a society in which power is exercised in the social production of a pattern of wants which can be satisfied without obstruction of the want-satisfaction of the power-holders is a conceptual possibility, but one that is at best (or, rather, worst) realised only partially. In most societies wants are articulated by broad sections of the population which, persistently for some minorities and occasionally for majorities, remain unsatisfied. Detectable conflicts arise around these wants, which sometimes take on a pattern incompatible with the prevailing 'pluralist' accounts of the distribution of power. The connection of empiricist and behaviourist research with 'pluralist' conclusions about the distribution of power is, therefore, purely contingent, and likely not to be universal.

Now, there arise several serious problems for the radical critic of such apparently 'legitimating' power research. First, it has to be shown that the social processes whereby wants are formed are appropriately described as involving power relationships. Second, if the critique is to sustain its political sting, then it has to be further demonstrated that the alternative patterns of wants are both possible and preferable. Third, if power relations are to be specified in situations where exercises of power are not identifiable in terms of observable acts or decisions of specifiable actors, then some alternative social ontology and epistemology has to be presented and defended.

In a moment I shall turn to a more detailed investigation of the ways in which contemporary Marxists and radical non-Marxists (both of whom are committed to rendering investigable as aspects of power the processes whereby wants and aspirations are formed) cope with these difficulties. First, though, it is necessary to clarify the range of options available. As to whether power relationships are necessarily involved in the social processes whereby characteristic patterns of wants are formed, it seems to me to be just about coherent to suppose that these social processes are self-reproducing in such a way that they systematically benefit certain groups in society without any act of intervention by those groups or their agents to secure this result. An extreme form of structural determinism would be required to theorise the operation of such a system. If such a theorisation were true of any social system, then, the correlation between the outcome of the want-producing system and the purposes of those who benefit from it could not be said to be the *outcome* of any exercise of power on the part of the latter. It might, of course, be a *source* of power for them (e.g. the apparent satisfaction of the wants produced by the want-producing process might serve as a legitimation of the continuation of it, in the event of any challenge to this).

Alternatively, any account of such a system which explains its continuation or effectiveness as conditional upon occasional or regular intervention in the process by the actors who benefit from it or their agents must also, in my view, conceive its outcome as the result of an exercise of power. I shall return to this later.

It is on the question of the possibility and preferability of patterns of wants in the population which are at odds with the ones currently socially produced that the radical critics experience their greatest difficulties. On the possibility of alternative patterns of wants, historical and cross-cultural comparisons, seemingly a rich source of evidence, are limited in their usefulness by the controversial character of any systematic method of describing and classifying wants, as well as identifying them cross-culturally. On the other hand, the assumption of the universal fixity of wants which would be required if the practice of taking them as given for any specific investigation were to be justified seems to be most implausible. The greatest area of difficulty for the radical critic is, however, the defence of the claim that some special significance attaches to the class of wants – potential wants – which may be denied both articulation and satisfaction in the existing order of society and which, by that fact, will fail to register in empiricist and behaviourist research. Why, indeed, *should* research be required to register wants which from the standpoint of the radical critics themselves are recognised to be absent? The answer here must be that the wants, aspirations, etc., which are absent, are only so because of the prior exercise of power and/or operation of real social processes. Such exercises of power/social processes are themselves significant in that they block the occurrence of what would have been significant states or activities of actors who are subject to them. Significant in what way? If the answer is just that *different* states and activities would have resulted, then the critique loses its political sting.

For this reason, the radical critics generally introduce some method of ethically, politically or, sometimes, causally privileging these alternative states or activities. The argument may be that the unarticulated wants are the ones whose satisfaction would be in the interests of the actors concerned, there being a present conflict between their express (socially produced) wants and their real interests. Alternatively (sometimes, even, simultaneously) it may be argued that the potential wants, preferences, etc. obstructed by the currently prevailing social processes of want-formation would be ethically preferable in so far as they were the wants, preferences, etc. of autonomous agents. Here the *content* of the potential wants and preferences is irrelevant to the ethical weight of the critique: the important thing is that they are the wants and preferences of an autonomous agent. Thirdly, 'potential' wants, preferences, etc. may be causally privileged in the sense that the prevailing want-producing system is subject to a counteracting tendency for alternative wants to assert themselves. Such a tendency may be conceived as the result of mechanisms peculiar to certain social forms, or as an instance of the general tendency of universal needs to assert themselves, irrespective of the character of specific social forms.

With the possible exception of some variants of the last-mentioned strategy, the special significance which is attributed to wants, preferences, etc. obstructed by the prevailing social system is based on some prior ethical or political commitment, on an ideal of personal autonomy, of egalitarian and co-operative social life or of the fulfilment of some other desirable human potential. If it is held that such ethical or political presuppositions are necessary to the identification of power relations in the social formation of patterns of wants and preferences, then it follows that the radical critique of the dominant tradition in power research must abandon any claim to value-freedom on its own part. It seems that the radical critique has two options only here. It may readily concede this, and argue for the unavoidably value-committed character of the terms of political discourse, so that the debate between the dominant tradition and its critics resolves itself into a dispute about the evaluative basis of each. Such contestations may, then, be expected to be irresolvable, the concepts in dispute being 'essentially contested'. The alternative would be to assign some form of objectivity to the value-standpoint of the radical critic, as against that presupposed in the research of the dominant tradition. Such a claim may take various forms, such as a teleological theory of the historical process which has the instantiation of the given values as its outcome, a theory of universal needs which incorporates those values as characteristically human or, possibly, biologistic, naturalistic, religious or mystical theories which provide some external or transcendent standpoint in terms of which particular social forms may be compared and evaluated. As we shall see, combinations of these two principal strategies are also possible.

Viewed from the standpoint of the dominant tradition, however, the refusal (on the part of the radicals) to take as 'given' the existing pattern of wants and preferences also has undesirable and even dangerous ethical and political implications. *Ex hypothesi* the radical critique is committed to the claim that the real interests, true needs, etc., and the potential wants whose satisfaction they would be, are quite other than the wants and satisfactions which are currently experienced by and available to the population. An analysis made on this basis could be expected to issue in policy prescription, then, ostensibly on behalf of and in the interests of the population, but against its express wishes. Since the political values of the radical critics are, generally speaking, egalitarian, democratic and/or libertarian, they are caught in a paradox: if they are to remain true to their political values they may implement no changes without the consent of those who are affected by them, and if they seek to implement no such changes, then they acquiesce in the persistence of a social system radically at odds with their political values. This paradox I shall call the paradox of emancipation. Its theoretical and practical solution is of great importance for Marxist and non-Marxist radicals alike. For Marxists, the attempt to combine a recognition of the domination of the consciousness of the subordinate classes by the ideas of the dominant class with a democratic practice of socialist struggle has always been a central strategic problem.

Finally, in this survey of the difficulties faced by a radical approach to power research, I shall mention the requirement that an adequate alternative be constructed to the behaviourism and empiricism of the dominant tradition. In what follows, I shall argue that the leading non-Marxist radical critics of that tradition have limited the effectiveness of their critiques by their failure to provide satisfactory alternative ontologies and epistemologies. The best-established alternative to empiricism has been some form of neo-Kantian dualism, and, particularly in the thesis of the indispensably value-laden character of the concepts of political analysis, this influence is very marked in the work of the non-Marxist radical critics, and in some of their Marxist colleagues. The emphasis on the importance of the social meanings of actions, and therefore on the value of interpretation, as distinct from empirical verification of external correlations, is also a feature of dualism, as is a reluctance to pursue a rigorously causal analysis of the conditions of action, and a commitment to individual actors and their actions as constituting at least the primary ontology of the social world. Taken together these features of the implicitly dualist epistemology and ontology of the radical critics obstruct the effectiveness of their critique. This is at the root of their unhappy confinement to a choice between cognitive relativism and ethical objectivism, their difficulty in specifying an empirically interpretable conception of power and their difficulty in consistently sustaining a conception of the structural conditions of power relationships.

Within the various Marxist traditions, the situation is more complex, and correspondingly more confused. Epistemologically, both empiricism and dualism are advocated by different traditions in Marxism. There is, in addition, an increasingly thoroughly articulated realist epistemological strategy. On ontological questions Marxists have been unanimous in denying the ontological primacy of the individual subject and his or her acts, but have been far from unanimous in their advocacy of alternatives. For some, the fundamental social realities are collective subjects, constructed on the model of a philosophical conception of the individual actor, whilst for others the primary realities are social structures of which (individual or collective) actors are mere 'bearers'. Various intermediate positions are also advocated.

3 *The concept of power*

Steven Lukes argues that there is a 'primitive notion' lying behind all talk of power – this is the notion 'that A in some way affects B'. But any way of conceiving power, to be useful in social analysis, must distinguish significant from non-significant 'affecting'. Lukes shares with another radical critic, W. E. Connolly, and with the one- and two- 'dimensional' views of power he criticises, a common concept of power, 'according to which A exercises power over B when A affects B in a manner contrary to B's interests' (Lukes 1976, p. 27).[2] In my view Lukes is quite right when he argues that it is this definitional link between power and interests which renders the concept of power value-dependent, and 'essentially contested', the relevant values being, of course, different ones, depending on the account of interests which is offered.

But even in the account of interests which he offers, Lukes is not far removed from his opponents. Whereas they, roughly speaking, define interests in terms of the actual pattern of felt

[2] For examples of what Lukes calls the 'one-dimensional' view of power, see Dahl 1961, Merelman 1968 and Polsby 1963. For examples of what he calls the 'two-dimensional' view, see Bachrach and Baratz 1962, 1963 and 1970.

wants, articulated grievances, express preferences, etc., Lukes himself defines interests in terms of the wants, preferences, etc. that actors *would* exhibit under conditions of autonomous choice. I shall criticise this conception of interests later, but for the moment I shall examine its implications for the view of power defined in terms of it. First, it should be noticed that Lukes defines power in terms of its exercise. Having power, as distinct from exercising it is, presumably, having the *capacity* to affect someone else (some other group, etc.) in a manner contrary to their interests. Lukes's way of defining power gives us no alternative to an analysis of this capacity in terms of what the possessor of power would do under certain circumstances. In short, power attributions are on this account a species of hypothetical, or conditional, statement. The possession of an unexercised power can be characterised only by means of a counterfactual conditional statement. But the identification of interests with the class of wants, preferences, etc. exhibited under conditions of autonomous choice adds a further element of conditionality to the analysis of power. *Ex hypothesi*, if power *is* being exercised, then the relevant wants, preferences, etc. are not exhibited under conditions of autonomous choice. Power attributions are doubly conditional, and essentially involve counter factual conditionals. Furthermore, as I shall argue later, there are reasons for supposing that the 'conditions of autonomous choice' involved in the definition of power are empirically uninterpretable.

If these features of Lukes's view of power are taken together, they seem to me to be more or less decisive against it. On the other hand, what I take to be the core of the radical critique of the dominant view(s) of power – the specification of power relations undetectable in the terms of such research – remains convincing. The question now becomes, is it possible to construct a concept of power which:

(*a*) is capable of allowing for the possibility, and sustaining analyses of the power relations involved in the social production of wants, preferences, etc.,
(*b*) sustains an empirically interpretable distinction between the possession, unexercised, of a power, and its exercise and
(*c*) avoids the value-dependence derived from any conception of in-

terests, and the further disadvantages attaching to the conceptions of interests advocated by Lukes, Connolly and other radical critics?

It seems to me that such a conception of power is possible, that it must be realist,[3] in that it contains a categorical element (the analysis of this concept of power would not, in short, be exhaustively conditional or dispositional), that it takes 'power to' to be a prior notion to 'power over' and that it dispenses with any definitional link with the notion of interests. Such a conception of power could be analysed as follows:

'A has the power to achieve A's objective' means 'A has capabilities and resources such that if A utilises these capabilities and resources, A will achieve A's objective' or, more briefly, 'A has the power to O_A' means 'A has C_A and R_A such that if A utilises C_A and R_A, A will O_A'.

In the above analysis 'A' represents a social actor of some kind or other – perhaps individual, perhaps collective. 'A's objective' or 'O_A' may be any state of affairs which A sets out to bring about, or wishes to occur. The categorical elements in this analysis of power are represented in the concepts of 'capability' and 'resources'. In the case of individual actors 'capabilities' will include knowledges, skills, competences, strength, etc., whereas in the case of collective actors 'capabilities' will include states of internal organisation, morale, availability of knowledge, skills, etc. of component individual actors, lines of communication, quality of leadership, etc. On the other hand, 'resources' of actors (individual or collective) will include those sources of power derived not from the intrinsic nature of the actor, but from his, her or its relationships to other human beings, collectivities and material things (legitimate authority, access to means of mass communication, control over means of coercion, possession of land, buildings, means of production, etc.). In the above analysis 'has resources' stands in for a great variety of relationships to a great variety of extrinsic sources of power.

One great advantage of this realist analysis of social powers is

[3] I derive this idea of what a realist conception of power amounts to from Harré and Madden 1975 but, where they provide an account of 'human powers', I have attempted to distinguish a category of 'social powers', which presuppose but are not reducible to human powers. The analysis which follows is of social powers: see Benton 1981, p. 175.

that it does allow of an empirically interpretable distinction between the possession and the exercise of power. If we know that A has *exercised* the power to achieve 'O_A', then this realist analysis points research in the direction of discovery of the basis for this exercise of power in the intrinsic capabilities of A, in conjunction with A's relationship to extrinsic resources. If, on the other hand, we know something of the capabilities and resources available to A then we already know that much about A's powers, irrespective of A's actual exercise of them.

The analysis must be supplemented, of course, if it is to take account of power *relationships*, in which A's power to achieve A's objective(s) implies a power *over* some other actor, or group of actors, 'B'. As opponents of the 'zero-sum' conceptions of power have correctly argued, A's power *to* does not *necessarily* involve power *over* B. This is only so where A's achievement of A's objective (O_A) is incompatible with the achievement by B of B's objective (O_B). It may be that A wants to make money, whereas B just wants peace and quiet. A's 'power to' achieve this objective would involve no 'power over' B, unless A's chosen method of making money (the source of his power to make money) is erecting an engineering factory next to B's house. In the latter case, A's achievement of O_A will depend on the comparison between capabilities and resources mobilised by A as against the capabilities and resources mobilised by B in pursuit of peace and quiet (knowledge of planning law and procedures, persuasive skills, understanding of relevant patterns of social relationships, access to press, councillors, appropriate political parties, financial resources, relationships with neighbours, etc.).

To cover such cases, where A and B cannot simultaneously attain their objectives, so that achievement by A of A's objectives implies power over B, the above analysis can be expanded as follows:

A has C_A and R_A, such that if (B has objective O_B *and* A utilises C_A and R_A) then (A achieves O_A).

Since A's power to achieve O_A under these circumstances may require A's overriding the full utilisation by B of B's resources

(R_B) and capabilities (C_B), we may expand the analysis thus:

A has C_A and R_A and B has C_B and R_B, such that if (B has objective O_B *and* B utilises C_B and R_B *and* A utilises C_A and R_A) then (A achieves O_A).

This analysis of A's power over B with respect to objective O_A has the merit of displaying the basis of that power in the capabilities and resources of A relative to those available to B. It allows of the attribution of this power to A even where either or neither of A or B actually utilise their abilities or resources. Unfortunately, however, it also allows of the attribution to A of this power over B even where B does not have objective O_B (as defined above, such that B's achievement of O_B rules out A's achievement of O_A). This might be thought to be not a serious problem. For Lukes it might even look like an advantage. After all, for Lukes it is important to have a concept of power which enables A's prevention of B's *acquiring* O_B *as* an objective to be described as an exercise of power. But in allowing for this the above analysis *also* allows for A's power to achieve O_A to count as power over B even where B simply does not take O_B as an objective, irrespective of the position, abilities or actions of A. In other words, the analysis fails to distinguish a 'spontaneous' consensus from one which is the result of the operation of power differentials.

What one does about this is to some extent simply a matter of terminological convenience, so long as the distinction between the various possibilities can be clearly made. One option is to retain the analysis as it stands, treating the relative resources and capabilities of A and B as a sufficient basis for the ascription of a power of A over B with respect to O_A. Where a mobilisation of resources or exercise of abilities on the part of A is required in order to prevent B's adopting O_B as an objective, this would count as an *exercise* of the relevant power over B whereas, in the absence of such mobilisation or exercise on the part of A, A could still be said to *possess*, unexercised, the relevant power over B.

Another alternative would be to shift 'B has objective O_B' from the antecedent to the consequent of the conditional in the analysis, which would now read:

'A has power over B in respect of O_A' means 'A has C_A and R_A and B has

C_B and R_B, such that if (B utilises C_B and R_B *and* A utilises C_A and R_A) then (B has objective O_B *and* A achieves O_A)'.

On this version of the analysis, A's power to achieve O_A only counts as a power over B if B actually adopts O_B. It can be saved from a tendency to collapse towards the one-dimensional view by a 'Gramscian' interpretation of objectives. If the criteria for saying that B has objective O_B are that B articulates an explicit demand for O_B, that it becomes an issue between A and B, then it is impossible on this version of the analysis to describe A's power to prevent B's articulation of objective B *as* a power over B. On the other hand, if the unarticulated symbolic content of B's practical struggles can be taken into account in attributing objectives to B, then A's power to prevent the articulation of these, and their emergence as issues between A and B, *can* be identified as a power of A over B.

Yet another option would be to replace 'B has objective O_B' as it appears in the last version of the analysis with 'O_B is a *possible* objective for B'. This would allow for the situation in which B in *no sense* adopts O_B as an objective, but *might* have to be described as one in which A has power over B. The meaning of 'possible' here has to be defined rather closely, though. What is required is a notion of 'theoretical' possibility such that theoretical assumptions plus knowledge of B's situation are sufficient to predict what B *would* want if it were not for A's power over B. In defining the working class, for example, Erik Olin Wright argues that certain locations 'structurally support' a socialist consciousness (Wright 1978, p. 94 n.). Irrespective of the truth or falsity of such a causal theory, it would be required if this version of the analysis of the concept of power were to be empirically interpretable.

The great advantage of this sort of analysis, I contend, is that it allows for the possibility and analysis of the power relations involved in the social production of wants, preferences, etc. ('objectives'), but it does so without making use of any ethically or politically contentious conception of interests. Whereas Lukes, Connolly *et al.* distinguish between the significant affecting of B by A (exercise of power) from trivial affecting, in terms of the supposed 'interests' of B, I do so in terms of the *objectives of A*. This not only dispenses with the concept of interests, but is liable to be empirically more fruitful in that it prompts the questions whether, why and for what purposes A requires 'power over' B. A crucial element in the intelligibility of the *dynamic* of a power relationship is restored in this analysis. The result is a thoroughgoing causal account of power, which satisfies the three criteria of adequacy outlined above.

Now, it may be objected to this conception of power that, whilst it may satisfy these criteria, yet it does not satisfy a further, and crucially important, criterion: it cannot allow for fundamental *shifts* in the power relations between A and B. If, it may be argued, A and B are assumed to utilise their capabilities and resources in whatever conflict develops between them, then the outcome is predictable and unvarying. Where the causal weight of A's combined resources and capabilities is greater than those mobilisable by B, then A achieves A's objectives. How is this consistent with change in the power relations between A and B? The answer to this is that the analysis so far presented simplifies power relations rather drastically, but that the analysis, without major revision, is quite capable of supplementation to take account of the possibility of changing power relations and, indeed, to illuminate important aspects of such changes.

We have so far dealt with A's power over B with respect to A's objective O_A, which is assumed to be incompatible with B's achievement of O_B. Any real power relationship will be far more complex than this in a number of respects. First, other individual or collective agents, C, D, E, each with their resources, capabilities, etc., will stand in a variety of relations to A and B, and are likely to have effects of various kinds on the resources available to A and/or B, the ability of A and/or B to deploy those resources, and the *commitment* of A and/or B to deploy their resources. If this conception of power were, for example, to be employed in the analysis of a persistent and pervasive power struggle, say, class struggle, then these complicating features of the analysis would figure in any attempt to account for patterns of class alliance.

Another area of complication is that, of course, A and B can be expected to be simultaneously in pursuit of a multiplicity of objectives. Not only may the power differential between A and B be different with respect to different objectives, but A and B will both be committed to an order of priorities among their objectives which will affect the extent to which either is committed to the full mobilisation of resources in pursuit of any one objective. Finally, it is important to recognise that among the objectives sought by A and B may well be items that, if achieved, will figure among the capabilities and resources available for deployment in the next 'round' of conflict between A and B or, if not achieved, will constitute a *depletion* of such capabilities and resources. In each of these ways, then, the basic conception of power I have outlined can take account of, and analyse, changes in the strategic balance between individual and/or collective agents engaged in persistent but shifting power struggles.

4 *Concepts of interests*

I have attempted to dispense with the definitional connection between 'power' and 'interests', partly because of what I take to be the necessary value-dependence of the concept of interests, and partly because of other difficulties which seem to attend the use of the concept of interests in this connection. I propose next to present an analysis of the concept of interests, which is designed to show that attempts to avoid what I have called the 'paradox of emancipation' by revising the concept of interests in such a way that actors are the sole arbiters of their own interests, necessarily fail. Conversely, though, I propose further to show that attempts to construct concepts of 'real' or 'objective' interests, *detached* from actors' own judgements, cannot attain the standards of objectivity and/or scientificity which they frequently claim. The concept of interests is, I shall argue, essentially contested, and simultaneously evaluative and cognitive. It belongs to a range of discourses and social practices which must be analytically distinguished from any prospective practice of scientific political analysis.

As I have already indicated, W. E. Connolly and Steven Lukes concur both with one another, and with the tradition of political research they criticise, in the necessity of definitional links between 'power' and 'interests'. But they have more in common than this. For all of them interests are identified with wants, preferences, etc. of actors. For the dominant tradition of power research, interests are empirically identified as currently expressed or felt wants or preferences. For Lukes, interests are identified with a privileged set of wants and preferences: those exhibited under conditions of 'relative autonomy ... e.g. through democratic participation' (Lukes 1976, p. 33). For Connolly, 'policy x is more in A's real interest than policy y if A, were he to experience the results of both x and y, would choose x as the result he would rather have for himself' (Connolly 1974, p. 64). For both writers, the main value of such a way of interpreting the concept of interests is that it allows them to maintain a critical distance from the prevailing pattern of wants, preferences and consequent choices and simultaneously to avoid the ethically and politically dubious claim to know the interests of others better than those others can know their own interests. In short, the attempt is to avoid the 'paradox of emancipation' through the device of according to actors the status of *ultimate* arbiters as to their own interests, whilst provisionally withholding the status of *immediate* arbiters.

On such analyses as these, then, it is the requirement that interests be self-ascribed by actors, albeit under special conditions, that is supposed to guard any use of such a conception of interests to legitimate tyranny: the implementation of policies against the express preferences of an underlying population, but purportedly in their interests. But the device is not successful in this, for in precisely the range of cases for which the concept was devised the situation is *ex hypothesi* not one in which actors' wants, preferences and choices can be regarded as identical with their interests. Where the exercise of power has been involved in the formation of current wants and preferences then, clearly, they are not the wants or preferences of autonomous agents. In the case of Connolly's proposed analysis, *ex hypothesi* the situation is one in which the agent conceived has, *in fact*, not had the opportunity to experience the results of both policies.

For precisely that range of cases, then, for which this type of analysis is produced, the judgement as to *which* class of wants, preferences, choices, etc. *does* constitute the interests of an actor who is subjected to an exercise of power has to be made by the external observer or analyst *on behalf of* the actor. The judgement that has to be made is how the actor would feel or behave under conditions which do not now hold, and maybe never have held, nor ever will hold. No matter how well-intentioned the observer, this is still other-ascription of interests, and not self-ascription.

But the situation for Lukes, Connolly *et al.* is still more serious than this, for it is the view or conception of interests which they deploy, not the agent concerned, that specifies the conditions which are privileged for the attribution of interests. In addition to the obvious problems about how the specified conditions are to be empirically interpreted (e.g. what *constitutes* relative autonomy?) there are further questions about the grounds on which this or that set of conditions for the expression of preferences, choices, etc. is privileged over any other set for the purposes of interest-ascription. Clearly these grounds are not incorrigible. As Grenville Wall rightly argues, it is still possible to hold that, even when an actor has experienced the results of a multiplicity of policy options, the policy that is chosen may still not be in the best interests of the actor (Wall 1974). Implicit in Connolly's analysis is a set of assumptions about human nature – that human beings can be mistaken about their interests only through lack of experience, and that experience necessarily corrects these mistakes, for example – which can be challenged. Similarly with Lukes: why are conditions of relative autonomy the ones which are chosen? Presumably because Steven Lukes is committed to a view of human agents such that the exercise of free choice is an essential property, and the facilitation of free choice is always in an agent's best interests.

There is, I suspect, little, if anything, which either Lukes or Connolly would disagree with in all this. They recognise that their conceptions of interests are value-dependent, and my linking of their conceptions with the conceptions of human nature and potential which they presuppose only serves to make this more explicit. But what is problematic for them in the above argument is that it shows yet another respect in which interests are necessarily other-ascribed, even on their own analysis. Not only is it necessarily an external observer or analyst who makes the judgement as to what the actor would do under certain (counterfactual) conditions, but it is also the external observer who decides (through the choice of conception of interests) which among the infinitely large class of counterfactual conditions are to be the privileged ones. Further, in so far as this judgement presupposes a value-commitment to one or another conception of human nature and potential the paradox of emancipation asserts itself once more.

At this stage in the argument, the only way of guarding against the legitimation of tyranny would be to disclaim any special status for the values underlying the chosen conception of interests; to embrace, in other words, some form of moral relativism. Both Connolly and Lukes seem, with some qualifications, to accept this option, in stressing the essentially contested character of concepts such as 'interests'. The obvious difficulty with this, though, is that it greatly weakens the force of the critique of the dominant tradition in power research. If there is no decisive case for accepting the value-perspective of the radical critic, and if the value-perspective is essential to the radical critique, then the case against the dominant tradition cannot be decisive. Lukes adopts an interesting compromise position in arguing that certain value-perspectives (in his case, a 'radical' one) carry with them a cognitive privilege. In some sense, one can see deeper and further into a society from some value-perspectives than others. As a matter of fact, I agree with this, but it seems to me that it doesn't help Lukes at all, since there remains the further question about how this thesis is itself to be established. Are there objective tests by which the cognitive superiority of certain value-standpoints can be assessed, or is this claim itself subject to the relativity of a value-standpoint?

Two further criticisms of the 'wants under privileged conditions' conception of interests are required for the further development of my argument. The first of these criticisms concerns the rather special nature of the counterfactuals involved in the attribution of interests, so defined, where the pattern of wants, preferences, choices, etc., of the agent concerned is the outcome of a process of social production involving power relationships. Such social processes are the mechanisms whereby individual human beings are constituted as self-conscious participants in forms of social life. The formation of a characteristic pattern of wants, preferences, objectives, etc., is a fundamental aspect of the overall formation of personal and social identities and identifications. There are important respects, therefore, in which to speculate as to what an actor might do, or might have done, in the absence of such processes is to ask an incoherent question. In the absence of *any* form of socialising practices, it is hard to see how social actors could be said to express preferences or make choices in any recognisable sense at all. If, on the other hand, we are to imagine the outcome of socialising practices which are radically reorganised and quite different from the ones with which we are familiar (both the Connolly and the Lukes analyses of interests require at least this) then it is hard to see how it would be appropriate to speak of the *same* actor as author of the hypothetical preferences, wants, etc. Certainly, we can imagine the same biological organism subjected to these different processes of social constitution, but in the relevant aspects of personal and social identities, this biological organism is the hypothesised material support of two quite distinct hypothetical social beings. If it is argued that we can, indeed, imagine one person, as a result of major historical change, or migration, undergoing such a transformation in the span of one lifetime, then this can certainly be conceded. But the question now is, what would be the grounds for privileging the newly acquired identity over the former? Connolly's assumption, for example, seems to be that there is a connection between a greater range of experience and a greater ability to judge one's interests. It could just as easily be argued that such a range of experience may dull the sensibilities, and lead to a loss of judgement.

The second line of criticism directly takes on the conflation of 'interests' with 'wants', 'preferences', etc., in the work of Lukes and Connolly, as well as those they criticise. That this is a conflation is best illustrated by means of a series of disanalogies in the 'logical grammar' of the two sets of concepts. There are only rather exceptional and special respects in which it is possible to make a mistake about what one wants or prefers, but we often recognise ourselves and characterise others as being mistaken about our, or their, interests. Connectedly, in the case of wants, self- and other-ascriptions are made on quite different bases: I require evidence of some sort to discover what someone else wants but, in my own case, I just want whatever it is, without asking myself, observing my own behaviour, etc. There is no such difference between the self- and other-ascription of interests. Having weighed up evidence and considerations in the course of assessing my own interests, I may check my judgement by consulting someone else. Equally, having assessed someone else's interests, I may check my judgement against their self-ascription. Further, there are disanalogies in the susceptibility of wants and interests to moral evaluations. Wants, preferences, choices are straightforwardly assessable as morally blameworthy, desirable, etc., but the job of making sense of a claim that someone ought or ought not to have the interests that she or he has is much more complex. Either 'interests' here is being used in a different sense (what claims their attention, or their 'stake' or 'investment' in some enterprise) or an indirect moral appraisal is being made of the social situation or circumstances of the actor concerned. Finally, that there is a difference of meaning between 'preferences' and 'interests' is illustrated by the fact that it is not self-contradictory to assert one's interest in performing 'a', but preference for 'not-a'.

Of course, these differences may seem to rely for their force on a readiness to take ordinary language usage as an arbiter of such concepts and there is, surely, no reason why political analysis should not subject concepts to revision. Indeed, there is no such general reason, in my view, but in the present case there are, in the detailed argumentation presented above, specific reasons for rejecting this revision.

By contrast with Lukes *et al.*, Marxists of most varieties have been consistent in detaching the concept of interests from that of wants and preferences. The assumption has been that, in one sense or another, interests are susceptible of objective identification, quite independently of the 'actual' or empirical wants of those to whom interests are attributed. In some cases, it is supposed that 'real' or 'objective' interests can be 'read off', as it were, from the social or economic position of the agent, or class of agents. It is doubtful, however, whether these positions can themselves be defined independently of the ascription of interests. Sometimes such accounts are supplemented by counterfactual hypotheses concerning the potential preferences, etc., of the occupants of these positions under conditions of autonomy and/or full cognitive appraisal of their circumstances. These cases approximate to the positions of Lukes and Connolly. In yet other versions, historically or ethically transcendent standpoints are adopted as 'anchoring' a concept of real interests. Potential forms of human existence, types of human character or relationship are identified as the realisation of 'true' interests, by contrast with the false or manipulated forms of recognition of interests imposed by the prevailing social order. Where such transcendent standpoints are constituted by a historical teleology in which such forms of (socialist or communist) existence are regarded as the necessary outcome of the historical process, the implicit claim is that the 'objectivity' of the associated interest-ascriptions is guaranteed by the 'march of history' itself. In such cases as these it can, I think, be readily demonstrated that no remotely plausible or coherent conception of historical causality could provide such a guarantee but, instead, a philosophical schema which imposes upon history the requirement that it realises the values of the philosopher–historian. Even where a socialist (or libertarian, or communitarian, etc.) form of life is used as a mere standard of comparison, without commitment to its historical inevitability, the conditions of possibility for such a conception of interests include at least: (i) a coherent conception of a socialist (etc.) form of life, (ii) the demonstration that such a form of life is a real historical possibility and (iii) a thesis as to the preferability of such a form of life over and above the prevailing one.

Finally, in some variants of Marxist theory, interests are connected with a theory of universal human needs. The interests of individuals or classes are in the pursuit of satisfaction of real needs, rather than the wants, or 'false needs' induced by the prevailing social system. Again, it is highly doubtful whether any theory of universal human needs could be constituted in a way which avoided value-dependence.

My claim then, in short, is that however they construct the concept of interests, and whatever 'objective' or 'scientific' status they give to the concept, the various traditions of Marxism are committed to *views* of interests which share with those advocated by Lukes, Connolly *et al.* an irreducible value-dependence.

Among the features of the concept of 'interests' which are of special significance for my argument are the following:

(*a*) interests are distinct from wants, preferences, etc., or any sub-class of them;
(*b*) any view or conception of interests is indispensably evaluative, and therefore 'essentially contested';
(*c*) the logical grammar of interest-ascription assigns no special place to self-ascription, as distinct from other-ascription of interests;
(*d*) the assessment of interests, whether of oneself or of others, involves the evaluation of evidence and considerations of more than one type. Specifically, relevant *evidence* will include information about the present and possible future circumstances, personal and social identity, preferences and ambitions of the subject, whilst relevant *considerations* will include the application of moral, prudential and/or political standards and principles to those preferences, ambitions, circumstances, etc.;
(*e*) in so far as interest-ascriptions rest on what I have called '*considerations*' they are contestable, but not demonstrably true or false. In so far as they rest upon what I have called '*evidence*' they are both contestable and (in principle) demonstrably true or false;
(*f*) there are intimate conceptual links between interests and personal and social identities. In so far as an individual is socially constituted as a member of a family, for example, anything which has a bearing on the well-being of the other members of the family or on the relationships constituting the family also has a bearing on the interests of that person. In this sense the family is constitutive of his or her identity in such a way that evidence and considerations about the prospects, circumstances and moral character of the family are indispensable to any assessment of his or her interests.

5 *Interests, power and the paradox of emancipation*

These features of the concept of 'interests' fit it to play a multiplicity of roles in a variety of discourses and related social practices in which identities are formed and transformed, in which conflicts of loyalty are resolved, in which specific courses of action are urged or opposed and in which exercises of power are legitimated. The concept of 'ideological struggles' will be provisionally employed to characterise these discourses and practices. But certain of these features of the concept of interests – most notably (*d*), the indispensably cognitive *and* evaluative character of interest-ascriptions – presuppose another type of discourse: one which issues in characterisations of social positions, relations and their future possibilities. It is to such specifically cognitive discourse that, I argued above, the concept of power which I advocate belongs. The use of the concept of interests in ideological struggles of various kinds requires, but cannot be reduced to, the results of cognitive social and political enquiry.

But a further condition of possibility of the social practices and associated discourses which I have collectively labelled 'ideological struggles' is that the social production of wants, preferences and identities is an internally contradictory process. By this, I mean that it cannot be the case that the mechanisms which operate to produce a pattern of wants etc. in conformity with the purposes of those who hold power act without confronting, or even simultaneously producing, counter-tendencies. It is a condition of possibility of 'struggle' that opposition of some form persists. A woman who has been socially constituted as a member of a family and identifies with her position and role within that family may also, through contact with feminist ideas and organisations, come to acquire partially or even wholly conflicting identifications, and so come to deploy a new conception of her interests which, under at least some circumstances, may issue in courses of action inconsistent with her identity as a member of a family. Similarly, an employee who has come to identify himself/herself and therefore his/her interests with his or her firm, and simultaneously with his or her workmates and their union, will experience a deep-rooted conflict of loyalty, and even a 'crisis of identity' when called upon by either union or employer to perform actions inconsistent with the alternate nexus of identifications.

Such patterns of actually or potentially cross-cutting, interlocking or conflicting identifications, loyalties and locations of interests are the raw materials in everyday life which provide the essential 'purchase' for the whole range of persuasive uses of the concept of interests. To attempt to persuade someone that one course of action, rather than another, is in their interests is to play a part in the social constitution and/or reconstitution of their social and personal identity. Ideological struggles are, in general, struggles over the constitution and incorporation of individuals into opposed patterns of social identity, loyalty and commitment, together with the interests that these carry.

Of course, such struggles are not exhaustively or exclusively 'discursive' in content. Rational persuasion, involving the use of concepts such as 'interests', is indeed one aspect of such struggles. But 'rational persuasion' shades off imperceptibly into more 'practical' forms of incorporation: involvement in the works' sports team, going with management to receive the Queen's award for industry, getting promoted, etc., versus mass meetings, election as a shop-steward, going on a trade union training course, learning to call your workmates 'brother' and 'sister' at branch meetings, and so on. The use of language, including the language of 'interests', is involved in all these activities, but it does not achieve its effects without the practical involvements and commitments with which it is interwoven.

Now, what I have called the 'paradox of emancipation' is resolvable only if what I have just identified as the conditions of possibility, in everyday life, of ideological struggle are really present. To be *persuasive*, oppositional uses of the concept of interests must be rooted in at least some aspect of the life-experience of those for whose identifications they are in competition. Otherwise they have no purchase, no relevance to their 'target' actors, and offer no means of active participation in the advocated shift of identity. Unless, then, the social form is one which simultaneously produces self-reproducing *and* self-dissolving oppositional patterns of social identification in at least some of its agents, the conditions of possibility of *persuasive* uses of the concept of interests for oppositional and emancipatory ends do not exist.

The range of persuasive uses of the concept of 'interests' and the associated mutual formation and development of oppositional socialising forms and practices (unions, movements, parties, associations, groupings and relationships of many kinds) collectively constitute what can be called 'democratic ideological struggle'. This is, in turn, to be regarded as an aspect of an overall democratic (but not in the limited and exclusive sense of 'parliamentary democratic') emancipatory and socialist political struggle, in which both organisational forms and forms of argument are among the capabilities and resources deployed in the struggle for power.

To deny, or to overlook, the counter-tendencies to the social production of consensual wants and identifications is to deny the possibility of ideological and political struggle which is simultaneously democratic and genuinely radical and emancipatory. It is to remain locked within a strategic perspective which offers only imposition of 'solutions' on an unwilling population, or feeble acquiescence in the *status quo*.[4]

REFERENCES

Bachrach, R. and Baratz, M. S. 1962. The two faces of power. *American Political Science Review*, 56, pp. 947–52.

1963. Decision and non-decisions: an analytical framework. *American Political Science Review*, 57, pp. 641–51.

1970. *Power and poverty: theory and practice*. New York, Oxford University Press.

Benton, T. 1981. 'Objective' interests and the sociology of power. *Sociology*, 15, 2, pp. 161–84.

Connolly, W. E. 1974. *The terms of political discourse*. Lexington, Toronto and London, D. C. Heath.

Dahl, R. A. 1961. *Who governs?* New Haven, Yale University Press.

Harré, R. and Madden, E. H. 1975. *Causal powers*. Oxford, Blackwell.

Lukes, S. 1976. *Power: a radical view*. London, Macmillan.

Merelman, R. M. 1968. On the neo-elitist critique of community power. *American Political Science Review*, 62, pp. 451–60.

Polsby, N. W. 1963. *Community power and political theory*. New Haven, Yale University Press.

Wall, G. 1974. The concept of interest in politics. *Politics and Society*, 5, 14, pp. 487–510.

Wright, E. O. 1978. *Class, crisis and the state*. London, New Left Books.

[4] This article incorporates substantial extracts from my earlier piece: Benton 1981. Some aspects of the argument I present here are given a more extended and detailed treatment in that version.

2 *The political status of children*

JOHN HARRIS

The political status of children in all societies reflects the almost universally held belief that children are incompetent to exercise the responsibilities and discharge the obligations of citizenship. This incompetence is the ground for their being systematically denied the dignity and status of adults. In addition to the long list of political and legal disabilities imposed on children – inability to vote, to initiate or defend legal proceedings on their own account, consent to sexual relations and so on – they are also positively controlled and their lives almost completely regulated by adults. They are in many respects their parents' dearest possessions and their freedom of choice, from the most personal item of clothing to what they may freely read or look at, from their living conditions to their choice of friends, is under arbitrary control. This control finds dramatic and public expression and reinforcement in the system of compulsory attendance at and obedience in schools.

While the supposed incompetence of children is the ground for the imposition of political disabilities, the control is justified by the belief that without it children will, because of their incompetence, do themselves various sorts of mischief and prove less able, or less quickly or thoroughly able, to shed their incompetence and qualify as adults.

Now, the idea of the incompetence of children and the disabilities that go with it presupposes that there is a range of capacities without which full political status cannot or ought not to be (safely?) granted. Is there such a range of capacities? Do we know what they are? And if we do, are we sure that children lack them and adults possess them?

In what follows I shall argue that the traditional distinction between adults and children, which incapacitates children because of their supposed incapacities, does not in fact distinguish adults and children. It may distinguish the competent from the incompetent, but if full political status is to be granted only to the competent, then a large and significant proportion of children must be granted full political status and a very great number of adults must be disenfranchised. If this conclusion is to be avoided we must find some account of the capacities relevant to self-determination which avoids the elitism implicit in our current assumptions. I shall end by trying to sketch such an account, which I hope will prove at least morally sustainable if not politically appealing.

1

The belief that children are incompetent to be fully-fledged citizens has always been as convenient to adults as the control and protection of children has been believed to be good for the children. Shakespeare is among the many people to have exposed the deficiencies of simple assumptions about the incompetence of children. In *Richard III* the Duke of Buckingham persuades Cardinal Bourchier that the young Duke of York has no right to claim sanctuary because:

> The benefit thereof is always granted
> To those whose dealings have deserved the place
> And those who have the wit to claim the place.
> This prince hath neither claimed it nor deserved it,
> And therefore, in mine opinion cannot have it
> . . .
> Oft have I heard of sanctuary men;
> But sanctuary children ne'er till now. (Act 3 Scene 1)

Buckingham's appeal here is to competence and perhaps rationality. Children are not competent to engage in the sort of dealings which the 'holy privilege of blessed sanctuary' traditionally protects; neither have children enough wit (or rationality) to make out a case for the privilege being extended to them, and so for both reasons may legitimately be denied its protection. It is this combination of competence and rationality that I will call the 'capacity criterion'. If this criterion is intended to be an empirical one, Buckingham is clearly mistaken on both counts. In as much as the princes were capable of having deadly political enemies, their dealings certainly 'deserved the place'. As events proved, they not only 'deserved' sanctuary but badly needed it. As for 'hav[ing] the wit to claim the place', both princes did in fact claim the place and were so well provided with wit that Gloucester says of the Prince of Wales: 'so wise so young, they say, do never live long' and of the Duke of York: 'O 'tis a parlous boy; bold, quick, ingenious, forward, capable' (*ibid.*).

Bold, quick, ingenious, forward and capable young people are by no means a rarity, neither, unfortunately, are dull-witted, incompetent adults. If freedom from control and full political status are things that we qualify for by the acquisition of a range of capacities, then as soon as anyone possesses those capacities they qualify, and if they never acquire them they never qualify. So if it is supposed that it is the comprehensive possession by adults of capacities lacked equally comprehensively by children that sustains and justifies the political disabling of children and the rule of adults, the supposition is false. False because there are numerous children whom it would be implausible to regard as incompetent and numerous adults whom it would be implausible to regard as anything else. Whatever we may finally decide about the status of children it is unlikely that the 'facts of human development', in so far as they are ascertainable, will support the rigid 'age of majority' division between adults and children. However, the myth that such facts as there are do support the traditional division is useful from many different perspectives, as we shall see. It is not perhaps surprising then that two[1] prominent recent writers on the status of children, while calling in question the justifications that are standardly produced for such a division, end by endorsing the *status quo*. The deficiencies of their accounts do, I think, help us to see both the different motives for supporting the traditional division and the reasons why we cannot succumb to the temptation.

Arguing from a strong libertarian position, Schrag (1977) presents arguments against the traditional rigid distinction between adults and children. He follows Shakespeare in showing

[1] One such writer mentioned here only in this note seems content with the present arrangements but questions the obligation of children to abide by them: see Haydon 1979; see also Brandon 1979.

that the 'facts of human development' do not support such a distinction and that if the arguments that are supposed to underpin the distinction were carried through consistently they would support the emancipation of many children and the disqualification of many adults. He then rehearses an alternative utilitarian account of the status of children, arguing that paternalism maximises the happiness of children who, even if they possess the capacity to make decisions for themselves, will still make disastrous errors through inexperience and limited understanding. This emphasis on experience and understanding rather than on powers or faculties is supposed to make plausible the setting of a similar date of emancipation to that set by the traditional account. Traditional childhood allows just sufficient time for us to acquire enough experience and understanding to deploy successfully our capacities in making the decisions that would prove disastrous but for that experience and understanding or, failing that, but for paternalist guidance.

But this account is vulnerable to the very arguments Schrag has already successfully deployed against it. For unless we learn from our experience it won't help to promote happiness; and in this context 'learning from experience' just means not making the sort of mistakes that lead to misery. And similarly, 'understanding' must here mean simply knowing how to avoid such mistakes. But here again whether or not such understanding has been achieved will be a question of fact, and again many children will be able to make successful decisions and many adults will not. And worse, as Schrag points out, 'can we not imagine farsighted individuals able to recognise that much that we do now is not merely injurious to others and to future generations but shortsighted in just the same way – that in twenty years we will profoundly regret the choices that we have made . . .' (Schrag 1977, p. 175).

This point of Schrag's emphasises what is perhaps a general truth; that paternalism not only tends to produce and justify elites, but tends to produce and justify a hierarchy, perhaps even an infinite regress of elites, each more farsighted and competent that the last, and each using this (fact?) to justify its rule over all those less well endowed.

But Schrag's account also serves to remind us that we adults are hardly in a position to claim much in the way of expertise at the difficult business of making wise choices. We do not need very farsighted individuals to point out to us that much of what we do now 'is not merely injurious to others and to future generations' but also shortsighted in that we will regret it later, if not already. Would any rational person who could plausibly claim the ability to learn from experience, or claim to possess whatever it is that is supposed to distinguish adults from children, smoke cigarettes, or allow the proliferation of private motor transport with its huge toll of death and injury from accidents and its profligate waste of scarce resources? Would the rational go to war 'to gain a little patch of ground that hath in it no profit but the name'[2] or over differences of religion that have even less profit? Or produce enough nuclear weapons to kill the entire population of the world many times over? I don't suppose everyone will agree with the items on my list, but what is significant is that everyone could produce, without hesitation, an equally disastrous catalogue of their own.

We don't of course know what disasters children would add to any of our lists. But if the avoidance of disaster is our top priority perhaps we should all be elitists. But, if elitism is unacceptable, perhaps we should be willing to pay a little more (or perhaps a little less?) of the same coin that we are already paying, to see that justice is done, that rights are not violated and that our policies are consistent with the arguments that purport to sustain them?

So both of Schrag's alternatives license paternalism for many adults and emancipation for many children. It is ironical then that Schrag, after agonising between them, chooses the traditional account. He does so for the surprising reason that he is reluctant to undermine 'a powerful bar to the encroachment of paternalism into our lives' (Schrag 1977, p. 177) – surprising because he has successfully shown that *both* accounts must inevitably license the encroachment of paternalism. Schrag of course partly sees this and ends by saying that perhaps his position amounts to supporting a 'noble lie', but believes this is redeemed by the fact that 'if so it is not one in which a few

[2] W. Shakespeare: *Hamlet*, Act 4 Scene 4.

deceive the masses for their own good, but rather one in which we *all* believe for our *own good*' (*ibid.*). The point that Schrag astonishingly misses, and to which we will return, is that many children don't believe it. And we should not perhaps overlook the possibility that the reason that they don't believe it is the simple and sufficient one – that it isn't true.

In a critical reply to Schrag, Scarre (1980) finds the paternalist conclusions which embarrassed Schrag broadly tolerable on utilitarian grounds. Indeed he produces an account of the circumstances under which paternalism is justified which would license the most comprehensive paternalist intervention:

> the paternalist should intervene in an individual's affairs only when there is reason to believe his decisions are not based on rational considerations, and that they are likely to result in a diminution of his stock of existing good, or under-achievement of his possible stock of good. (Scarre 1980, p. 123)

Despite being a good utilitarian I don't suppose that I am alone in being painfully aware of how many of my own decisions are not based on rational considerations. Moreover, of that lamentably high number of my decisions which either diminish my stock of existing goods or, more likely, result in my under-achieving, many *are* the result of rational considerations! And this even on Scarre's somewhat circular (for his argument) account of rationality. For Scarre there are two hallmarks of rationality:

> rational actions are those which are directed to maximising the expected utility of the agent. In addition, actions backed by rational decisions typically manifest themselves as elements of a systematic approach adopted by the agent for maximising his good. (*ibid.*)

So, what looked like two tests for the justification of paternalism collapse into one, since acting rationally and being a utilitarian with respect to one's own good turn out to be one and the same. I am unhappy with Scarre's narrow account of rationality which seems to make self-sacrifice, lack of competitiveness and modesty, etc., irrational, but I will not pursue the point, since my present difficulty is with the use Scarre makes of his account.

Scarre just assumes that children and adults are separated one from another by the presence and absence of 'rationality':

> The ability to plan systematic policies of action is essential to solving the practical problems of living. Most adults, because they have lived a long time, have this ability, but children, because their mental powers and experience are alike inadequate, do not. Hence adults must impose a comprehensive 'system of purpose' on them. (*ibid.*)

Scarre then takes the case of the alcoholic whose decisions are neither rational nor well calculated to maximise his utility, and comments:

> The reason why we cannot carry the alcoholic away for a fortnight's forcible cure, even though his drinking is harmful and is not sanctioned by his reason, is that by doing so we should insult him by imposing our plans for his life on him when, as an adult, he has plans and policies of his own. Children do not have such systems of purpose of their own, so it does not infringe their rights to intervene in their behalf when their irrationality threatens their well-being. (*ibid.*)

Scarre concludes that anyone believing in individual rights must agree never to allow paternalist interventions in the affairs of those who 'in general manifest the ability to consider their actions rationally' (*ibid.*).

It is far from clear, as Scarre assumes, that all or even most children do not have the ability to plan systematic utility-enhancing projects of their own; and it is farther from clear that those who do not have such an ability would not rapidly develop it if permitted, or forced by the experience from which adults protect them, so to do. They might not of course have quite *the same* conception of utility as most adults, but it is not clear that the mismatch would be any more vicious than that between the conceptions of utility possessed by eighteen and eighty-year-olds!

Scarre would have to show that children do not or cannot have a *plausible* conception of the good, not that we do not share their conception, or that they will regret the conceptions they now have, or cease to hold them, when they are our age. I now regret many of the things I did and the priorities I had and the plans I made when I was eighteen, but my present regret, or change of heart or mind, is no evidence that the decisions and plans of my youth were irrational. Nor does it mean that I would have, nor yet that I ought to have, welcomed paternalist interference from Scarre, on the grounds that he foresaw what perhaps I too then realised, that I would think differently about my priorities when I was older.

Again, Scarre's position requires that he can show that children have *no* ability to plan systematic policies for achieving their ends, not merely that, like the rest of us, children do not always plan the most efficient policies and sometimes make unrealistic plans.

What then is to count as evidence of the ability to plan 'systematic policies of action' or as the ability to solve 'the practical problems of life'? If getting what you want counts as one of the practical problems of life (and if it doesn't, it's difficult to imagine what does!), then any child who works out strategies for achieving this, whether by crying or nagging or pleasing or whatever, is doing very well on the Scarre criterion. If it is objected that in these sorts of cases the child is reliant on others for the achievement of his goals rather than being self-reliant, then I wonder if any of us are self-reliant in the requisite sense? For who can say that the realisation of their desires is entirely independent of the will of others, let alone the brute forces of nature?

If the criterion is to turn on the more demanding requirement that an individual be able to master the complex techniques required for living and operating in the modern world, then again it looks as though very many children would qualify and very many adults would not. But what is to count as a legitimate technique for these purposes? Perhaps the most crucial technique is the ability to get others to do things for us. Can we relevantly distinguish achieving this by the payment of money or by an exchange of goods or services, or by the expedient of an appearance of helplessness, if they all, equally well, get the job done? If an appearance of helplessness is thought illegitimate in some way we must remember that it is by no means only children who have mastered this valuable technique. Indeed, in reality children are more apt to claim expertise than to be content to appear helpless.

Is the objection rather that, whether or not children appear helpless, they actually *are* helpless? Again this will be a question of fact in each case, but the idea of helplessness is not without its difficulties. Is the adult who needs the help of all sorts of experts to function adequately in a complex world to escape the charge of helplessness? Most adults need the help of lawyers, doctors, nurses, accountants, bankers, mechanics, electricians and so on to maintain even a modest existence. If helplessness is to carry the sort of weight that would be sufficient to disqualify children, then whatever conception is used, it should be such as to allow us to recognise when individuals have ceased to be helpless and to recognise those that never do. Of course we do recognise, care for and politically disqualify some helpless adults, but only very young children are as helpless as these! I will say something about an appropriate age for majority in the next section, but for the moment it is perhaps enough to note that if helplessness is to be our criterion of competence then we should have a coherent view of helplessness and only disqualify those who qualify.

But since only very young children and very few adults will be *comprehensively* helpless, we will need to talk about helplessness with respect to particular projects, and to have a view about the sorts of projects that are somehow associated with moral and political competence.

Perhaps it will be objected that it is not helplessness broadly conceived but rather children's inability to act as any of the sorts of expert listed above. But again this will be a question of fact in each case, and clearly false as a general thesis. Many children are first-rate mechanics and electricians, not to mention musicians, athletes and so on, and but for age-disqualification could begin the process of qualifying for other professions like medicine and the law long before the present age of majority. The fact that many would not complete the training until a long time past this age is no more an argument against their liberation, than the same facts are arguments against adults being liberated until the age at which they could reasonably have qualified, or actually do qualify, for the most demanding of occupations.

But even if *no* children had enough expertise to help us or each other with the problems of living, we would still be left with the problem of distinguishing between adults on this ground. For although 'adults', as the class of all adults, can clearly be experts of any sort, many numerous sub-classes of adults are not experts of any sort, and others could at best only be experts of some limited sorts. The criterion is neither workable nor sensible but, in so far as it could be coherently applied, it would liberate many children and disqualify many adults.

If Scarre fails to render children vulnerable to paternalism, he also fails to protect adults. The rule for the protection of adults is: no interference with those 'who in general manifest the ability to consider their actions rationally' (*ibid.*). But for Scarre the point of rationality, indeed its essence, is to maximise utility: so why in the case of the alcoholic who acts both irrationally and against his own best interest should we not be paternal, why should the fact that in *other* areas he is rational protect him from the self-defeating irrationality of alcoholism? After all if, as Scarre stresses, 'the amount of a person's happiness is the key consideration in determining whether he is to be subjected to paternalism' (*ibid.*)[3] then it would be irrational for Scarre to hold back here. But this of course *is* the thin end of the wedge.

A point that plays an important part in Scarre's account is the view derived from Dworkin (1977) that it is wrong to insult someone by imposing our plans for his life upon him when he has plans of his own, wrong because to do so is to treat him as less than an equal, it is to deny him the same concern and respect that is accorded to those we do not insult in this way.[4] It is substantially the same point as that made by Oscar Wilde when he attacked his critics with his definition of selfishness: 'Selfishness' Wilde remarked, 'is not living as one wishes to live, it is asking other people to live as one wishes to live.' If Scarre could show that children are not the sort of beings capable of being insulted in this way and that they do not have the right to be shown a concern and respect equal to that which adults deserve or can command, then perhaps the paternal status of adults would be assured. But many children do have plans of their own and are insulted. It is difficult to think that the degree of insult is proportionate either to the quality of the agents' plans or to their

[3] Amy Gutman, in a recent 'liberal' defence of paternalism, adds the demand that we respect only 'settled' preferences. The idea of respecting only non-capricious adults, while interesting, is not likely to recommend itself to liberals: see Gutman 1980, p. 340.

[4] See especially Dworkin 1977, ch. 6.

appropriateness, or congruence, with the agents' other wants or needs.

However it is dressed, the capacity criterion fails to distinguish between adults and children since, once again, many children have the relevant capacities and many adults lack them. When H. L. A. Hart observed in passing that: 'The parent's moral right to obedience from his child would I suppose now be thought to terminate when the child reaches the "age of discretion"' (Hart 1967, p. 63), he assumed both the capacity criterion and that some respectable conception of moral obligation could be founded on it or at least defeated by it. Certainly the idea that children do have a moral obligation to obey their parents and to attend school during the working day is of great utility to adults. Perhaps, though, it would be more realistic to regard this situation as resulting from the exercise of naked power by adults, and to think of the status of children as a consequence of their losing out in the perpetual struggle between the generations in power and the generation seeking power.

2

This rather cynical view of child–adult relations, which sees schooling as a sort of compulsory national crèche giving adults freedom during the working day, while it may be nearer to the truth than many accounts, is certainly unsatisfactory. I want now to sketch a positive account of the status of children which places most children in the same class as the rest of us when it comes to being deserving of equal concern and respect; and which argues that the crucial distinction is not that between adults and children but that between persons and non-persons. This dividing line, as will appear, does not fall in a place that would justify the traditional disqualification of children.

It is unlikely that we live on the only populated planet in the universe. When and if we encounter beings from other worlds we may be met not only with fascinating scientific data but also with moral claims. Suppose we found creatures naive in comparison with ourselves but who have lives of their own to lead and who tell us (when we have learned their language) that they wish to be left alone to lead those lives in their own way. We may see at once that if we were able to have charge of their education for a few years (say ten) we could teach them how to avoid many things that at present they regard as natural and inevitable calamities. Maybe we could vastly increase their present and their expected utility. Perhaps they could even be brought to see that all this is so and so have a reason to accept education from us. But what if they still want to lead their own lives in their own way, to make their own mistakes and learn from them in their own (slow by our standards) good time? They do, after all, have the ability to plan their own futures and solve (or learn to live with) the practical problems of living. It's just that they're not anywhere near as good at it as we are. What they insist on is that it's *their lives* and they wish to live them *their own* way. They claim that it is insulting for us to impose our plans on them when, as self-conscious autonomous language-users, they have plans of their own.

In a wonderful book, William Golding (1955) describes a society of Neanderthal people, much more primitive than the creatures we have just imagined and much more naive than most children. They are not tool-users, they are not capable of abstract thought and, indeed, their reflective powers are confined to what they can or cannot picture in their mind's eye. They have a language, but not one that enables them to overcome the limits imposed on their self-consciousness by what they are able to picture. They might find it difficult to make out a case, that is to say, to formulate or articulate a case, to be left alone if discovered (as they were) by the likes of us. But their gentle loving society as described by Golding makes their case for them. It is difficult, having glimpsed their simple and co-operative society, to be confident that ours is so vastly superior as to justify our imposing it on them if we could. Certainly they could learn much from us and, almost as certainly, we would not learn anything we didn't already know from them. But if this is to be the test for a justified paternalism, then democracy, except for a small 'guardian' class, is dead.

Suppose the extra-terrestrial beings we discovered had discovered us, and were as much our superiors in technology, foresight and rationality (in Scarre's sense) as we are to our children or to the beings imagined above. What if they announced a programme of ten years' compulsory 'education' for us, after which we would be left alone again, but would be changed irrevocably? We might see the advantages as well worth the price, but what if we did not? What if we were inclined to argue that we, like they, are sentient rational creatures with plans of our own and who value, among other things, the freedom to make our own mistakes and the dignity of devising our own conceptions of the good life? These may not be as efficient or as trouble-free as those we might be taught to devise or which others might devise for us. But one of the things we value (irrationally?) about them is that they are *our own*. And we might not even mind being taught to devise better ones if we were free to choose whether to be taught or not, and free to contract out if we didn't like the way things were going.

If we value people, and if we are committed to a conception of equality which protects a person's dignity and independence by requiring that each person is shown the same concern and respect as that shown to any, then we need some account of who is valuable and who is protected by the principle. It would be parochial in the extreme to suppose that adult human beings were the only qualifiers. But even if they (we!) turned out to be the only ones with the appropriate *curriculum vitae* we would still require some account of what qualifications were relevant to full political status. We may be required to consider the claims of creatures, perhaps simpler than ourselves, on other planets and we may be anxious that beings more sophisticated than ourselves would recognise our own claims. (It may be that both animals and machines may be making such claims of us in the not-too-distant future.)

How then do we recognise beings as people? What is it about people which persuades us or ought to persuade us that they are worthy of the same concern and respect that we show to one another? I think the features to which we are responsive and which make our concern and respect appropriate are those which allow us to think of other beings as creatures who value their own lives. It is difficult to know quite what this involves but I suppose that at the very least it would involve such a person having a conception of their life as their own – that they had a life to lead and valued leading it. To get even this far a creature would have to be self-conscious, it would have to be aware of itself as an independent being existing over time and be aware of and be able to make sense of that awareness. Part of making sense of that awareness would be the sense that life was an enterprise over which it had direction and so it would be able to gain and revise an overall conception of its life and have a sense of how well it was doing in the light of that conception.

To have a life to lead, then, is to have decisions and plans to make and things to do, it is to be aware of doing it all, to understand roughly what doing it all involves and to value the whole enterprise. This self-awareness will involve some intelligence. What precisely is required here is notoriously difficult to specify but, again, I suppose it would include first the ability to discover that others too possessed these qualities and so valued their lives in the same way. The ability to see the connection between action (and inaction) and consequence, and some rudimentary understanding of the nature of the consequences, would also be required. Something as simple as awareness that certain features of the world are painful and dangerous and that other features are required in order to sustain existence would perhaps be enough. So for a world like ours the sorts of things I have in mind would be awareness that fire burns, knives and broken glass cut, roads are dangerous, not everything can be safely eaten and that these things hold good for others too. In short, the sort of knowledge that allows us to say that beings are responsible for their actions, the sorts of knowledge and awareness that make praise and blame appropriate.

It is difficult to imagine creatures able to do all this without also possessing a language which could act as the vehicle of thought, which would enable them to formulate their alternatives, make their plans and be aware of what those alternatives and plans are. A language would of course also enable them to learn that others were like themselves or enough like themselves to matter also. So perhaps possession of a reasonably rich language would be a good criterion of personality. It would of course have to be a language sophisticated enough to enable them to do all this, a language properly so called. But this, while vague, is a reasonably low threshold.

My point is that if we take seriously the question: 'To whom is equal concern and respect owed?' and if we think carefully about the sort of things to which we are responsive when such claims are considered, it would be difficult in the extreme to except children without excepting all but the most exceptional of ourselves. Children, that is, who are reasonably competent language-users, who have wants for themselves and their future which they can plan plausibly, not necessarily most successfully, to achieve and who are reasonably responsible for their actions.

If we are looking for an age at which to set the emancipation of children, 'ten' would be a more likely candidate than 'eighteen'. But given what is at stake, are we entitled to continue to be so arbitrary about the age of 'majority'? We must remember that to deny someone control of their own lives is to offer them a most profound insult, not to mention the injury which the frustration of their wishes and the setting at naught of their own plans for themselves will add. Perhaps we should conduct annual examinations from an early age to be sure that we do as little of this sort of damage as possible?

The alleged 'fact', which is used by Scarre and others to justify the total violation of the right of young persons to be shown equal concern and respect, is the prospect held out by James Fitzjames Stephen that 'if children were regarded as the equal of adults . . . it would involve a degree of cruelty to the young which can hardly be realised even in imagination' (Stephen 1967, pp. 141–2). Is this true, and if it is, is it a greater price than is already consequent upon the emancipation of adults?

This spectre raised by Stephen is well calculated to induce failure of nerve, but in one sense it is unexceptionable and in another irrelevant. If Stephen is taken to mean that unless children *are protected from* adults they will be cruelly used, then this might be true but need not concern us. For a principle of equality *is* a principle of protection. If children are genuinely regarded *as the equals of* adults, then they are regarded as being entitled to equal protection, as being entitled to be shown the same concern and respect as adults. To regard people as equals is precisely to recognise that they are not equally able to protect themselves, or further their own interests or are necessarily the same in any other sense. It is because of inequalities that people are in danger of arbitrary and ill usage, tyranny, exploitation and so on. To regard people *as equals* is to take a stand on how they are to be treated, not to make a remark about their capacities. It is to recognise that they have something about them which justifies their being accorded the same status as others irrespective of their ability to achieve that status for themselves.

One might more plausibly argue against Stephen that it is precisely because children have been treated as children and not as equals that they have been fair game for adults, exploited, abused, tortured and arbitrarily done to death.[5] And irrespective of the merits of their case for equality of concern and respect, we should grant children this status merely out of paternalistic concern for their welfare.

But what would it be like to treat all children who were people, all competent language-users say, as equals? First, we are not simply to imagine that children would be emancipated, not forced to go to school, permitted to vote and to work, etc., and that all else would remain the same. How things would change will depend in part of course on the children, but we needn't suppose that one consequence would be that they would be left without education and so without the chance of improving their all-round competence (if that is what education does). Nor does it mean that they would necessarily be exploited in the labour or other marketplaces. There may be a parallel here with the treatment and status of the aged and retired, the so-called 'senior citizens'. They have full political status and remain citizens with citizens' rights, but with generally reduced opportunities for work, reduced income and increased (but not debilitating) dependence. Perhaps there is a case for creating some sort of 'junior citizen' status for children with citizens' rights, but with reduced opportunities for work and increased opportunities and incentives for undertaking education (but not compulsion). It is surely not absurd to suppose that we could arrive at something far short of the horror envisaged by Stephen. Perhaps this sort of status would enable us to treat children as equals while recognising their special needs. Or perhaps it would highlight the deficiencies of our provision for the elderly?

We must remember too that full political status for all persons

[5] For an exhaustive catalogue of the ill-use of children, see de Mause 1976.

does not mean that age cannot continue to be a relevant criterion for some purposes. We might continue to think that the possession of firearms and the freedom to drive dangerously powerful or large motor vehicles might usefully be made age-dependent without significant loss of political dignity. Neither will we be barred from continuing to regard experience and qualifications which take a long time to acquire as relevant criteria for admission to certain professions, or to the holding of particular posts or to the gaining of promotion.

At the very least, though, the granting of full political status to all people will mean that they have the right *inter alia* to vote, to work, to initiate and defend legal proceedings, to own property, make wills, enter into contracts, be criminally responsible and have the right to due process of law.

It is perhaps salutary to remind ourselves here that the franchise, which is perhaps the clearest and traditionally most hallowed right of citizenship, has, since universal adult suffrage, made minimum demands on the intelligence and rationality of voters. The whole apparatus of voting, whether by making an X-shaped mark on a ballot form or by pulling a lever, is designed so that a child could perform it.

The granting of full political status to children would also affect family life, though how much and whether adversely or not is difficult to predict. The question will turn on how competing rights within the family are to be understood and resolved.

Distinguishing her position from that of Fried (1978), Amy Gutman has argued that:

> it is not because children are the physical appendages or by-products of their parents' personalities that parents are free to tell them what to eat, when to go to bed, and how much (or little) television to watch. Parents have these rights to discipline, educate and socialize their children (even where we have room to doubt that their chosen modes of discipline, education and socialization serve the best interests of their children) because parents also have a right to choose for themselves among competing conceptions of the good. (Gutman 1980, p. 353)

And so long as the parents conceive the moulding of their children as part of *their*, the parents', conception of the good life they are entitled to disregard their children's possibly different view of matters.

But, of course, parents can only be entitled to disregard the rights of their children on the assumption that they are competent to exercise free choice of lifestyle but that children are not. There is a difficulty with Gutman's position here, because she wants to hold that 'when a child is mature enough to distinguish his religious beliefs from those of his parents, his beliefs ought to be consulted' and yet she seems to want to leave room for their utter disregard, for she continues: 'yet one might still justify placing those restrictions upon his present freedom of action that serve both to develop his rational capacities and to expand his future opportunities' (*ibid.*, p. 355). Gutman admits to unease here but takes comfort in the thought that 'it is worse to restrict children's future opportunities against their will than it is to force them to keep their future options open' (*ibid.*).

She believes that the position she outlines and defends:

> establishes a middle ground of freedom for adolescents: granting them free exercise of rights against certain attempts to restrict their future opportunities (by limiting their education) but not against educational requirements that serve to expand these opportunities. At the same time my position is compatible with the view that there are other situations in which no plausible paternalistic grounds exist for restricting the free exercise rights of adolescents. In these situations a liberal state may be required to limit the paternalism of parents without substituting its own control over adolescents. One might argue for example that the state is obligated to respect and protect the rights of adolescents to express their political and religious beliefs, read whatever literature they wish . . . (*ibid.*).

Now this is at severe odds with Gutman's defence of the freedom of choice of lifestyle for adults, a point she notes without quite noting its seriousness for the structure of the argument. Gutman defends parental control on two grounds; one is paternalism and the other the right to free choice of lifestyle for adults. Paternalism is justified on the grounds of expansion of future opportunities for children, an argument which, as we have noted, makes impossible the rational relinquishing of such control at any time prior to death. However, parental control is not justified by paternalism alone so that when, as Gutman suggests, the state limits 'the paternalism of parents' it does not undermine the grounds of their supposed legitimate control. For the right to such control is part of the parents' right to free choice of lifestyle.

But the dilemma which then faces us is not that put by Gutman. It is not that 'it may be difficult for the state fully to protect adolescents' rights without violating parents' personal freedoms within the family' (*ibid.*, p. 356). This implies that we are comparing parents' full rights as persons on the one hand with children's rather specific and limited rights to certain protections for specific purposes on the other. Whereas in reality we are here faced with competing and incompatible rights to free choice of lifestyle.

One way of dealing in law with this situation might be to extend to children who are also persons the right, only recently established for spouses (whether common law or 'legal'), to common ownership of the family home. It would then be a home in which all members of the family had an equal stake. While there would certainly be an extension of the legal rights of young persons within the home there is little reason to suppose that this would mark the end of family life or lead to a state of perpetual family litigation. People would have to decide whether they most prefer life within the nuclear family or along some other lines.

It is worth recalling that a host of similar disasters were all predicated upon the recognition of equal status for women within marriage, the family and the home. But there is little evidence that more radical equality for women has made marriage and family life impossible. Where there is protection from tyranny it is more difficult to tyrannise. We should perhaps be encouraged by the fact that the same list of disasters and warnings about dire consequences for life as we know it was raised as an objection to the emancipation of women and to all subsequent extensions of equal rights to them as is now produced to defend the continued control of children.

One consequence of course will be that, just as people have been forced to relinquish conceptions of the good life which necessarily involve their controlling the lives and attempting to control the thoughts and beliefs of others, they will have to come to accept that they must abandon such conceptions which require that children be forced to share their parents' beliefs and practices whether they wish to or not.

While it is impossible to predict with any confidence what precisely would be the consequences of emancipating children, we have plenty of evidence about the emancipation of adults, which cannot be counted an unqualified success. No rational person in Scarre's sense would, as we have seen, concur in the private use of motor transport, let alone its use by anyone under the age of thirty-five. The death toll and hospital register hardly allow us to think of private motor traffic as a utility maximiser. Neither would 'rational' people smoke, eat rich food, fight for justice against the odds, indulge in high-risk pastimes or, as in the United States, permit the private possession of firearms. This is a bag of very mixed blessings. My point is not to challenge or to champion the freedom to any of these but to point to the following dilemma.

If we believe we should show equal concern and respect for persons it is hard to define 'person' in such a way as to exclude any but the youngest children. The justification of paternalism lies in the desirability of the reduction of vicious mistakes. It would be absurd if one class could become licensed, by something as arbitrary as chronology, to make such mistakes and another not, especially if this does not in fact much reduce such mistakes and is certainly not the fairest or otherwise best or most efficient way of reducing them.

The alternatives seem to be these: if we are serious about protecting people from the consequences of their stupidity, shortsightedness, recklessness and so on, then egalitarian democracy is absurd and we should have the courage to be full-blooded elitists. If, on the other hand, we believe in something like equal concern and respect for all persons, then we have to have a way of recognising persons when we encounter them. If we make our criteria too demanding we will find that we have arrived at elitism via another route. The conception of 'personality' that I have suggested yields a non-'speciesist' account of what it is to be a person with an easily applied criterion of recognition – all reasonably competent language-users will qualify. This does not of course mean that *only* reasonably competent language-users will qualify. Where we have reason to suppose that beings, while not possessing language (or not giving evidence of such a capacity), are nonetheless self-conscious beings, aware of themselves as existing over time and valuing existence, then we will have reason to include these creatures as well.

There would still be the category of foetuses, babies and young children who had not yet achieved full political status, and perhaps another class of adults who through severe disability had ceased temporarily or permanently to be persons. Both of these groups of human non-persons would have political disabilities. This does not of course mean that they are 'fair game', without rights, nor does it mean that persons do not have responsibilities for them. Quite what the moral and political status of human and other non-persons is must be a task for another occasion. I do not see however that the disqualification of adults who had ceased to be persons could be anywhere near as worrying as the disqualification of children, and many mental patients, who are clearly persons.[6]

REFERENCES

Brandon, E. P. 1979. The key of the door. *Educational Philosophy and Theory*, 2, pp. 23–34.

Dworkin, R. 1977. *Taking rights seriously*. London, Duckworth.

Fried, C. 1978. *Right and wrong*. Cambridge, Mass., Harvard University Press.

Golding, W. 1955. *The inheritors*. London, Faber and Faber.

Gutman, A. 1980. Children, paternalism and education: a liberal argument. *Philosophy and Public Affairs*, 9, 4, pp. 338–58.

Hart, H. L. A. 1967. Are there any natural rights? In *Political philosophy*, ed. A. Quinton, pp. 53–66. Oxford University Press.

Haydon, G. 1979. Political theory and the child. *Political Studies*, 27, 3, pp. 405–20.

de Mause, L. 1976. The evolution of childhood. In *The history of childhood*, ed. L. de Mause, pp. 43–9. London, Souvenir Press.

Scarre, G. 1980. Children and paternalism. *Philosophy*, 55, pp. 117–24.

Schrag, F. 1977. The child in the moral order. *Philosophy*, 52, pp. 167–77.

Stephen, J. F. 1967. *Liberty, equality, fraternity*. Cambridge University Press.

[6] Thanks are due to Keith Graham and to members of the Political Philosophy and Economic Theory Seminar at the University of Manchester for many helpful comments.

PART II

Human Ideals

3 *Liberal rights and socialism*

RUSSELL KEAT

1 *Introduction: capitalism, socialism and liberal democracy*

The view that there is some intrinsic connection between liberal-democratic political systems and a capitalist economy is one that has been shared by many theorists of both the left and the right. Thus, for example, whilst Lenin wrote that a '... democratic republic is the best possible political shell for capitalism, and therefore capitalism, once in possession ... of this very best shell, establishes its power so securely, so firmly, that *no* change of persons, of institutions, or of parties in the bourgeois democratic republic can shake it' (Lenin 1963, p. 296), Milton Friedman argues that only a free market economy, with minimal state intervention, can guarantee the preservation of individual rights and political liberties:

> Historical evidence speaks with a single voice on the relation between political freedom and a free market. I know of no example in time or place of a society that has been marked by a large measure of political freedom, and that has not also used something comparable to a free market to organize the bulk of its economic activity.
>
> (Friedman 1962, p. 9)[1]

This supposed link between capitalism and liberal democracy has been reflected in the way that many Marxist socialists have viewed these liberal rights with the greatest suspicion, in relation both to their function in capitalist societies, and their possible place in a socialist society. The suspicion is encapsulated in the phrase 'bourgeois democracy'. Conversely, opponents of socialism have tended to argue that one of its central defects is the impossibility of maintaining these rights in such a system, and have pointed to the experiences of, for instance, contemporary East European societies to support this claim.

[1] This apparent agreement between left and right is explored in Jessop 1978.

Recently this question of the relations between socialism, capitalism and liberal rights has emerged with considerable force in a number of areas of theoretical and practical engagement: in the attitude of the West European left to Carter's 'human rights' policies, and to the activities of political dissidents in the USSR and East Europe; in the Eurocommunism debates;[2] and in Britain, for example, in the attempts made by E. P. Thompson to 'steer the left' towards a major emphasis upon the significance of civil and political liberties.[3] It is my aim, in this paper, to examine one particular area of Marx's work that has an important bearing on many of these issues, his discussion in certain early writings, especially 'On the Jewish question' (Marx 1975), of the relations between 'civil and political society' – roughly, between the social relationships of a market economy, and the political institutions of a liberal-democratic state.

I choose this particular area partly because I believe it is liable to misinterpretations that can generate, and have generated, a misplaced hostility towards liberal rights amongst Marxist theorists; and partly because it has recently been used by a well-known critic of (certain features of) Marxism, Leszek Kolakowski, as the basis for claiming an inherent totalitarian tendency within Marxist theory. I shall shortly present the main elements of his argument, and go on to respond to it through a fairly detailed critical exegesis of 'On the Jewish question' itself. But first, a few more preliminary remarks.

Marx's analysis of the relations between civil and political society – and, in particular, his claim that the separation of one from the other must be overcome to achieve 'human emancipation' – is one, but *only* one, of the major elements in his work that is relevant to the overall question of liberal rights and socialism. Amongst others, there is the question of his view of the 'transitional phase', and the dictatorship of the proletariat; and also of his apparent attitude towards *any* system of (legal) rights as inherently bourgeois.[4]

I shall have nothing to say about either of these themes in Marx's writings; so in this, and no doubt in other respects, my

2 See, e.g., Carrillo 1977.
3 E.g. in some of his articles collected in Thompson 1980.
4 See, especially, Marx 1968.

focus is subject to very definite limits. Further, most of what I say will be tied to the interpretation of one particular text, and to evaluating Kolakowski's objections to its claims; though I will also suggest how, properly understood, these claims provide an important basis for criticising some central features of John Rawls's major work of liberal political theory (Rawls 1972). However, though I will offer little in the way of direct argument for this I should make clear my own political standpoint as it relates to the issues discussed. I basically support the conception of political rights and liberties characteristic of much liberal political writing and practice; and I see them as, historically, one of the major progressive features of capitalism, and as something to be preserved in the construction of a socialist order.[5] Preserved, but in a 'transcended' form: I use the Hegelian concept here, because I find it the most illuminating way in which the relationship between socialism and capitalism can be conceptualised, a point which I explore briefly towards the end of this paper. And I hope to show how this concept of transcendence operates, at least implicitly, in 'On the Jewish question', which is, I think, an exemplary piece of political theorising despite certain flaws.

So I begin with Kolakowski. In 'The myth of human self-identity' (Kolakowski 1974) he argues that the totalitarian character of many self-proclaimed 'socialist' societies is an inevitable consequence of any attempt to realise in practice a central ideal in Marx's early political writings: to overcome the separation of civil and political society.

Kolakowski says that Marx's basic conception of the relationship between civil and political society, as presented in these texts, persisted intact throughout his intellectual development, though it required some adjustments in the light of his later adoption of a class analysis. He implies that the ideal of the unity of civil and political society involves another unity, 'the perfect unity of the personal and communal life of every individual', which he defines as 'the perfect, internalized identity of each

[5] Here, as throughout, I do not try to distinguish 'socialism' from 'communism', partly, because I am suspicious of most ways the distinction is made or used, and also because I don't think it affects the level of analysis at which I am operating.

person with the social totality, lack of tension between his personal aspirations and his various social loyalties' (*ibid.*, p. 32). He argues that this latter unity is incompatible with the existence of those differences of interests and values that are (in his view) an ineliminable feature of social existence, and concludes that:

> The dream of perfect unity may come true only in the form of a caricature which denies its original intention: as an artificial unity imposed by coercion from above, in that the political body prevents real conflicts and real segmentation of the civil society from expressing themselves. This body is almost mechanically compelled to crush all spontaneous forms of economic, political and cultural life and thus deepens the rift between civil and political society instead of bringing them closer to each other. (*ibid.*, p. 34)

Thus Kolakowski believes that the absence of liberal-democratic rights in societies constructed self-consciously on Marxist principles is no 'accident', but an expression of certain aspects of Marx's political theory. Against this, I will argue that there is nothing in the ideal of overcoming the separation of civil and political society, as such, that has these practical implications; but that (and here I partly agree with Kolakowski) there are important defects in the way Marx characterises and criticises civil society, with potentially dangerous political consequences. First, though, we need a fuller account of Marx's claims.

2 *Marx on the separation of civil and political society*

Marx criticises Bruno Bauer's response to the demands being made by Jews in Germany for religious freedom (Marx 1975). Bauer, says Marx, had argued that what was needed instead was complete 'political emancipation' for *all* Germans. This political emancipation would involve the elimination of all political distinctions based on criteria such as birth, education, occupation and property, as well as religion; and Marx notes how, in the constitutions of some contemporary American states, considerable progress towards this had been made. But he then goes on to argue that political emancipation is not enough. It presupposes the separation of civil society from the state (or political society), and genuine '*human* emancipation' requires the overcoming of this separation. What precisely does Marx mean by this?

For Marx, following Hegel, 'civil society' consists of those areas of a society in which relationships are dominated by the conflicting interests and desires of '*private*', egoistic individuals, a Hobbesian *bellum omnium contra omnes*. In modern societies this includes, especially, economic relationships. By contrast, the political realm in these societies displays a quite different conception of social relationships. It is a '*public*' realm, composed of equal '*citizens*', and expressing the communal, species-being, of authentic humans. Marx describes the situation in modern societies (as compared with feudal societies, where the separation does not exist) like this:

> Where the political state has attained a full degree of development man leads a double life, a life in heaven and a life on earth, not only in his mind, in his consciousness, but in *reality*. He lives in the *political community*, where he regards himself as a *communal being*, and in *civil society*, where he is active as a *private individual*, regards other men as means, debases himself to a means and becomes a plaything of alien powers. (Marx 1975, p. 220)

However, Marx is concerned not merely with the fact that these two realms are separated, but with their relative significance in the actual, concrete existence of members of these societies. Here, the parallel with the contrast between 'heaven' and 'earth' is revealing: man's political existence is (almost as) unreal and 'abstract' as that in heaven, whilst in his real, earthly life, the relationships of civil society predominate. And Marx conceives of the overcoming of this separation in the following terms:

> Only when real, individual man resumes the abstract citizen into himself and as an individual man has become a *species-being* in his empirical life, his individual work and his individual relationships, only when man has recognized and organized his *forces propres* as *social forces* so that social force is no longer separated from him in the form of *political* force, only then will human emancipation be completed. (*ibid*., p. 234)

I think it is clear that the ideal presented here – which Kolakowski describes, perhaps rather misleadingly, as the *unity* of civil and political society – involves 'realising' the at present 'unreal' form of social relationships in the political state, by a reconstruction of the realm of civil society, so that it too manifests this form. In other words, what Marx wants to see is not the simple elimination of the modern political state, together with its various rights and liberties, but of a situation where the authentic, communal existence of humans is confined to a highly abstract realm of political society and citizenship. However, to support this interpretation, I need to say more about Marx's attitude towards political emancipation, and his view that 'man as citizen' is 'abstract'.

At several points Marx comments favourably, though with qualifications, upon political emancipation and the modern conception of the political state, in which everyone is to participate as equal citizens in the determination of public issues. He says, for instance: '*Political* emancipation is certainly a big step forward. It may not be the last form of general human emancipation, but it is the last form of human emancipation *within* the prevailing scheme of things. Needless to say, we are here speaking of real, practical emancipation' (*ibid.*, p. 221).

Further, he appears to include, amongst the positive features of the modern state, the existence of certain individual rights, namely the 'rights of the citizen' (*droits du citoyen*), which he is careful to distinguish from other such individual rights, the 'rights of man' (*droits de l'homme*), towards which he is highly critical. I will discuss later the significance of this distinction, and Marx's view of the 'rights of man', but for the moment will simply note his comments on the former. In clearly approbatory terms, he describes them as '. . . rights which are only exercised in community with others', and goes on: 'What constitutes their content is *participation* in the *community*, in the *political* community or *state*. They come under the category of *political freedom*, of *civil rights*, which as we have seen by no means presupposes the consistent and positive abolition of religion and therefore of Judaism' (*ibid.*, pp. 227–8).

The phrase 'as we have seen' refers the reader back to the preceding discussion of religious freedom during which, amongst other points, Marx discusses how some contemporary American states had abolished property qualifications, as well as religious ones, for political rights. He notes that this 'political annulment of private property does not mean the abolition of private property': in other words, the existence of suffrage rights that do not involve distinctions based on property ownership in no way implies the abolition of those distinctions, and their consequences, in the *non*-political sphere of civil society. The same goes for 'distinctions based on *birth*, *rank*, *education*, and *occupation*' (*ibid*., p. 219). Marx indeed makes a further claim in this passage, namely that the political state actually *presupposes* the existence of these 'distinctions', in civil society: I will return to deal with this in section 5.

Finally, Marx's favourable attitude towards political emancipation is indicated by the fact that he is clearly critical of the way that, amongst theorists of the French Revolution, the character of the political state is justified by presenting it as a means for the preservation of civil society and its 'rights of man'; for instance, in Article 2 of the 1791 *Declaration of the rights of man*, 'The *goal* of all *political association* is the *conservation* of the natural and imprescribable rights of man', which Marx quotes (with his own emphases), and comments upon as follows:

> we observe that citizenship, the *political community*, is reduced by the political emancipators to a mere *means* for the conservation of these so-called rights of man and that the citizen is therefore proclaimed the servant of egoistic man; that the sphere in which man behaves as a communal being (*Gemeinwesen*) is degraded to a level below the sphere in which he behaves as a partial being, and finally that it is man as *bourgeois*, i.e. as a member of civil society, and not man as citizen who is taken as the *real* and *authentic* man. (*ibid*., p. 231)

Given that Marx adopted this partly favourable attitude towards political emancipation and the rights of the citizen, what were the qualifications to this approval? These seem mainly to consist in his general claim that the political state, and its conception of citizenship, is 'abstract'. It is worth distinguishing several somewhat different elements in this claim, which are suggested at various places in the text.

First, political emancipation (and with it, the value of the political rights it establishes) is a highly limited form of human emancipation, because the model of human relationships it espouses, involving equality, participation and communality, is restricted to a single sphere of activity that represents a relatively minor part of people's lives. Thus Marx talks of '. . . the spirit of the *state* where man behaves – although in a limited way, in a particular form and a particular sphere – as a species-being, in community with other men' (*ibid.*, p. 221).

Second (and this is really the corollary of the first point), political emancipation is limited in that, in the vast spheres of social existence that are non-political – that is, in civil society – the character of human relationships is quite the opposite of that involved in political society. Here, there is inequality, egoism, the war of all against all: and it is in civil society that the major part of people's lives takes place. (I will be discussing Marx's characterisation of civil society later on.)

Third – though here the direct textual evidence is rather unclear – the nature of social relationships in civil society actually undermines the practical effectiveness of the alternative form of relationships in the political sphere itself. That is, it is not merely that political society is limited in its scope, but that even *within* it, its ideal conception of social activity is undermined by the character of civil society. For instance, Marx says of the political revolution through which the separation of civil and political society was achieved, that:

> it unleashed the political spirit which had, as it were, been dissolved, dissected and dispersed in the various cul-de-sacs of feudal society; it gathered together this spirit from the state of dispersion, liberated it from the adulteration of civil life and constituted it as the sphere of the community, the *universal* concern of the people IDEALLY [my emphasis] independent of those *particular* elements of civil life. (*ibid.*, p. 233)

The 'ideally' that I have emphasised suggests to me that Marx is here implying that this separation of the political spirit from the particularities of civil society was not altogether real; that, in practice, political life remained 'adulterated' by civil life.

3 *Marx's analysis as a critique of Rawls's liberalism*

In the preceding section I have been arguing, in effect, that when Marx rejects *political* emancipation in the name of *human* emancipation, he is proposing the extension and realisation of the conception of social relationships already expressed, as an ideal, in political society, and in which the 'rights of the citizen' are guaranteed. It is not that this conception is *itself* to be replaced by another, but that its 'abstract' character (in the senses I have tried to outline) is to be removed. Thus, *so far*, there are no grounds for believing that 'overcoming the separation of civil and political society' has the kind of practical implications, in terms of the undermining of political rights, that Kolakowski suggests. However, before going on to examine Marx's characterisation of civil society and 'the rights of man' – which does, I believe, provide *some* grounds for Kolakowski's claims – I will illustrate the significance of the aspects of Marx's analysis (Marx 1975) so far presented, by discussing some central difficulties in a contemporary political text (Rawls 1972).

In this work, Rawls proposes the following two principles of justice:

> First: each person is to have an equal right to the most extensive basic liberty compatible with a similar liberty for others.
> Second: social and economic inequalities are to be arranged so that they are both (*a*) reasonably expected to be to everyone's advantage, and (*b*) attached to positions and offices open to all. (Rawls 1972, p. 60)

Much of Rawls's book consists in the attempt to justify these principles, partly by showing that they would be chosen by rational, mutually disinterested individuals in a hypothetical 'original position', but this need not concern us here. Instead, I want to point out how the differentiation of the two principles – the former insisting upon equal liberties, the latter specifying the conditions under which inequalities of income, wealth, power, etc., can be legitimated – presupposes a separation between two spheres of society that correspond very closely to the political state and civil society. For, as Rawls himself puts it:

> As their formulation suggests, these principles presuppose that the social structure can be divided into two more or less distinct parts, the first principle applying to the one, the second to the other. They distinguish between those aspects of the social system that define and secure the equal liberties of citizenship and those that specify and establish social and economic inequalities. The basic liberties of citizens

are, roughly speaking, political liberty (the right to vote and to be eligible for public office) together with freedom of speech and assembly; liberty of conscience and freedom of thought; freedom of the person along with the right to hold (personal) property; and freedom from arbitrary arrest and seizure as defined by the concept of the rule of law. (*ibid.*, p. 61)

But this presupposition in fact proves to be highly problematic, in ways that Rawls only partly recognises, and with consequences that he is very unwilling to accept. To see this, we need to focus upon his conception of '*self-respect*'. Rawls defines self-respect, which he regards as the most important social good, as consisting in two elements: 'First . . . it includes a person's sense of his own value, his secure conviction that his conception of his good, his plan of life, is worth carrying out. And second, self-respect implies a confidence in one's ability, so far as it is within one's power, to fulfil one's intentions' (*ibid.*, p. 440). He rightly emphasises that, for people to have such self-respect, it is essential that they engage in activities and relationships in which their feeling of significance and competence is affirmed by others; and that this itself requires a mutual, reciprocated sense of equality.

Now, Rawls argues that self-respect will normally be ensured by the operation of the first principle of justice, which specifies equal liberties. Thus: 'The basis for self-esteem in a just society *is not then one's income share* but the publicly affirmed distribution of fundamental rights and liberties. And this distribution being equal, everyone has a similar and secure status when they meet to conduct the common affairs of the wider society' (*ibid.*, p. 544: my emphasis). But how is Rawls to justify the part of this claim that I have emphasised: why is it that people would not, in a Rawlsian society, find their self-respect related, not exclusively to their status as equal citizens, but also – or even, instead – to their relative position in the distribution of income, wealth or economic power? And if this were to be so, surely the inequalities legitimated in these areas by the second principle would serve, on Rawls's own account, to undermine self-respect, through the absence of reciprocally affirmed equalities?

Rawls eventually concedes that 'to some extent men's sense of their own worth may hinge upon their institutional position and their income share', and that inequalities otherwise legitimated by the second principle may have to be adjusted if the self-respect of the worst-off is undermined by them. He says though, that 'this problem is an unwelcome complication', and argues that such situations are rather unlikely to arise in practice (*ibid.*, p. 546). I cannot explore the reasons he gives for this (in his terms) optimistic view, though I think they can be shown to be inadequate.[6] What should be clear, however, is that this 'problem' indicates one important respect in which Rawls's conception of the division of society's basic structure 'into two more or less distinct parts' is both crucial to his theory of justice, and *prima facie* implausible.

But there is a further problem concerning this presupposed division. Not only may the inequalities of (Rawls's version of) civil society counteract and override the self-respect said to be generated by the equal citizenship of political society, but they may also directly undermine the equality of the rights and liberties constitutive of that citizenship. For, as Rawls himself recognises, inequalities of income, wealth and power may affect the degree to which different groups and individuals can make use of their formally guaranteed liberties, thus generating differences in what he terms 'the worth of liberty'. He says that '. . . the worth of liberty is not the same for everyone. Some have greater authority and wealth, and therefore greater means to achieve their aims' (*ibid.*, p. 204), and notes some of the potential dangers of the unequal worth of liberty: 'Political power rapidly accumulates and becomes unequal; and making use of the coercive apparatus of the state and its law, those who gain the advantage can often assure themselves of a favoured position' (*ibid.*, p. 226).

However, Rawls's attempts to deal with this problem seem inadequate. Instead of insisting that no inequalities otherwise allowed by the second principle should be permitted if they generate inequalities in the *worth* of liberty, he introduces what is, in effect, a compromise proposal, that what he calls 'the fair value' of political liberties must be maintained. This involves ensuring that '. . . those similarly endowed and motivated

[6] See Keat and Miller 1974.

should have roughly the same chance of attaining positions of political authority irrespective of their economic and social class' (*ibid.*, p. 224), a definition which, as he notes, is analogous to his earlier definition of the 'fair equality of opportunity'. And he mentions a number of measures which he thinks would be helpful in maintaining this fair value, such as the public funding of political parties and 'government monies provided on a regular basis to encourage free public discussion' (*ibid.*, p. 225).

Whether or not such relatively superficial measures could in fact ensure the fair value of political liberty (which I doubt), it is clear that they could not – and neither is it Rawls's intention that they should – ensure equality in the worth of political liberties. In this respect, then, the conception of citizenship in Rawls's theory of justice remains 'abstract' in a sense corresponding to the third element of this concept distinguished in my discussion of Marx (1975) in section 2. Likewise, my comments on his account of self-respect suggest that this displays the second of these elements. That Rawls's citizens are 'abstract' in the sense of the first element, I will not argue for here, though I think it can be successfully shown in a number of ways.

4 *Problems in Marx's critique of the 'rights of man': individualism v. community*

Having discussed Marx's account of the relationship between civil and political society, and his view of both the virtues and the limitations of political emancipation, I will now examine his critical remarks on the nature of civil society and the 'rights of man'. His general claim is this: 'The first point we should note is that the so-called *rights of man*, as distinct from the *rights of the citizen*, are quite simply the rights of the *member of civil society*, i.e. of egoistic man, of man separated from other men and from the community' (Marx 1975, p. 229). Clearly, Marx regards this claim as constituting a major criticism of these rights which, following Article 2 of the 1793 *Declaration*, he specifies as equality, liberty, security and property. I will argue, against this, both that Marx is mistaken in claiming that the rights of man are, necessarily, the rights of egoistic man, separated from others and the community; and also that his systematic use of 'egoism' as a critical, negative term indicates a normative framework which is seriously inadequate.

Marx argues that, of the four basic rights just mentioned, those of equality and security have little content independently of the other two, liberty and property. So he confines most of his remarks to these, and I will follow him in this, ignoring the others. He quotes two more or less equivalent definitions of the right to liberty, and in effect discusses the second, from the 1791 *Declaration*: 'Liberty consists in being able to do anything which does not harm others.' He then makes the following claim:

> The liberty we are here dealing with is that of man as an isolated monad who is withdrawn into himself . . . [it] is not based on the association of man with man but rather on the separation of man from man. It is the *right* of this separation, the right of the *restricted* individual, restricted to himself. (*ibid.*, p. 229)

This is surely mistaken. The right to liberty, as defined above, is the right to do anything that does not harm others. This in no way excludes activities which involve 'associations' with others. There is no presumption behind this right that any interaction between individuals is typically, let alone necessarily, harmful to one or another participant, so that only the actions of an entirely isolated individual could be free. All that is presumed, for this right to liberty to be relevant, to be worth having and enforcing, is that *some* activities that an individual may otherwise wish to engage in may have harmful consequences for others: not that *all* of them always will.

It is of course true that the degree of significance attached to this right to liberty is partly a function of how conflictual a view is taken of the typical character of relations between individuals or groups; and that those who regard this right as the primary foundation of the social order have tended to assume a highly conflictual model of 'human nature'. But support for the right to liberty does not presuppose this Hobbesian picture. It requires only that another (in my view equally mistaken) model is rejected, namely that of 'rational harmony', according to which an incompatibility of interests is necessarily a sign of some (in principle) eliminable defect in the rationality of either individual character or social structure.

Marx proceeds to link the right to liberty to that to property by saying: 'The practical application of the right of man to freedom is the right of man to *private property*' (*ibid.*). This seems to me misleading. For whilst it is true that in societies based upon private property, the exercise of the right to freedom will frequently involve property rights (though not always, since not every social relationship in such a system involves their exercise), it does not follow that only in these societies can a right to freedom be relevant. Thus, whatever the merits of Marx's subsequent criticisms of the right to property, they do not apply *ipso facto* to the right to freedom, as they would do if his claim quoted above were correct. So let us look now at these criticisms.

Marx takes the definition of this right from the 1793 *Declaration*: '"The right of *property* is that right which belongs to each citizen to enjoy and dispose *at will* of his goods, his revenues and the fruit of his work and industry"' (quoted, *ibid.*, p. 229). His initial comment is that this is 'the right of self-interest', to act 'as one wills, without regard for other men and independently of society' (*ibid.*, p. 229). Again, this is slightly misleading. For although the right to property clearly does protect this kind of activity, it is not necessarily the case that it will be exercised in only this way. Further, it may seem to be implied that any self-interested exercise of the right will be inimical to anyone else's interests, and this, as I shall shortly suggest, may not be so. But what is perhaps more important here is that Marx in effect 'misses an opportunity' for a different kind of criticism concerning the relationship between the rights to liberty and property: namely, that exercise of these two rights will tend to conflict with one another. For it can easily be shown, I think, that an economic system based on private property generates systematic 'harm' through exploitation.[7] That is, the exercise of private property rights (unless these are hedged around with such extensive qualifications as to render them practically meaningless) is incompatible with the maintenance of an (equal) right to liberty. It seems that Marx's near-identification of the rights to property and liberty excludes the possibility of this kind of criticism of the former by reference to the latter.

[7] However, it must be remembered that at this point in his development, Marx had not yet introduced the concept of class into his account of civil society.

Marx then goes on to claim that, taken together with the right to property, the right to freedom 'leads each man to see in other men not the *realization* but the *limitation* of his own freedom' (*ibid.*, p. 230). But it is hard to see why this should be so. Consider, for instance, property transactions involving legal contracts. Here, the two parties will typically regard each other's agreement as enabling them to do what they want and which, in the absence of the other party, they would be unable, or less easily able, to do. In this activity, then, each 'sees the other', not 'as a limitation', but 'as a realization' of their freedom.

However, an adequate assessment of this criticism would require examination of the conception of freedom that is operating here. For both in Marx (1975) and in other writings, it seems that Marx is unwilling to accept that the social relationships involved in (economic) *exchange* can properly be said to display genuine freedom. This is so, whether or not these exchange relationships include the sale of labour-power itself.[8] That is, Marx's view of the kind of communal, co-operative activities expressive of a realised human species-being is such that typical forms of mutual self-interest are excluded. I cannot go into this issue here; but some of my remarks in what follows may be relevant to it.

The frequency with which Marx describes the members of civil society as self-interested or egoistic and the absence, in these cases, of any further explication of the concept, indicate that he took this to be a serious condemnation of civil society and (what he regarded as) its rights (Marx 1975). I will suggest – though only in a very schematic and assertive fashion – that in doing this, Marx was mistakenly adopting a simple, mutually exclusive and exhaustive dichotomy between self-interested and other-interested motivations, whereas what he needed (and elsewhere partly approached) was a properly dialectical grasp of the (partly) progressive and valuable features of the egoism of civil society.

The danger in using egoism as a purely negative category is the implicit endorsement of altruism as its preferred alternative. For

[8] It follows that, for Marx, full human autonomy cannot be achieved in 'market socialism', since, despite the absence of class exploitation, alienation continues through the existence of exchange relationships.

this is to remain trapped in a form of 'moralism' in which any kind of self-concern is automatically rejected as morally unacceptable, and to take as one's ideal a society of selfless, other-regarding agents. Such an ideal does, of course, have the apparent virtue of guaranteeing co-operative harmony as the general condition of society; but at the cost, it could be argued, of any genuine differentiation and sense of autonomy amongst its individual members.

I will give just one example to illustrate some of what is at issue here. A recurrent criticism of socialist ideals of economic distribution, such as 'from each according to their ability, to each according to their needs' is that these are entirely impracticable, given the 'egotistic' nature of humans. Socialism, it is objected, requires of human beings a degree of altruism in their attitude towards work that is quite impossible to achieve. There are at least two responses that can be made to this. The first is to argue that egoism is not 'natural' to humans, but the product of a historically specific form of social existence; and that, with departures from this form, the necessary degree of altruistic motivation will readily emerge, with individuals working 'for the sake of the community', 'the revolution' and so on. The second challenges the assumption in the initial objection – which is in effect shared by proponents of the first response – that socialism requires the replacement of egoism by altruism. Instead, on this view, what is required are radical changes in the character and organisation of work itself, so that it becomes an activity that will be freely engaged in by self-interested individuals, because they find it intrinsically satisfying, and need neither special financial incentives, nor altruism, to motivate them to do it.

Needless to say, versions of both responses may well be combined: I do not present them as mutually exclusive. But whereas the former – in my view – remains trapped within the egoism v. altruism opposition, the latter may suggest that there is nothing in itself undesirable about the pursuit of self-interest, whilst of course 'reserving the right' to discriminate between acceptable and unacceptable forms of self-interest.

However, a fuller analysis of Marx's use of the concept of self-interest in the critique of civil society would require an adequate treatment of the historically changing character of the concept of selfhood itself, and particularly of the changes in this during the period of development encompassing feudalism and capitalism in Western Europe. For this is the period during which the set of values loosely grouped under the heading 'individualism' were developing; and this, of course, was related to changes in the character of social relationships (especially those influenced by the emerging market economy) which also involved changes in people's conception and experience of themselves as individual and social agents.[9] Indeed, as is often now pointed out, the term 'individualism' itself was introduced into the vocabulary of social and political theory by early nineteenth-century French conservative writers, such as de Maistre, in their opposition to the values and practices of the Revolution; and it soon became an important conceptual element in the European conservative critique of the developing market economy, and the consequences of the industrial revolution.[10]

If we place Marx's attitude towards civil society and egoism within this broader context of social and theoretical developments, we become aware of certain dangers in the use of these concepts. There are, after all, important parallels between his characterisation of civil society (Marx 1975), and the theoretical categories of conservative thought that emerge most systematically, later in the nineteenth century, in Tönnies's distinction between *Gemeinschaft* and *Gesellschaft*, 'community' and 'society' (or 'association'). The latter concept of the pair is taken to be most clearly exemplified in the contractual exchange relationships of the market economy: and it is Tönnies's claim that social relationships of this kind are coming to predominate in modern society, replacing those of *Gemeinschaft*–exemplified by institutions such as the medieval guild, or monasteries.

But it is crucial that any socialist opposition to the character of the social relationships of capitalism does *not* involve the essentially backward-looking, conservative critique of individualism and self-interest. It must instead take up a standpoint

[9] Two interesting interpretations of these changes are: Fromm 1960 and Trilling 1972.

[10] See, e.g., Lukes 1973 and Nisbet 1970 – an excellent account of the place of 'community' in nineteenth-century conservative thought.

(usefully, I think, termed 'dialectical') that emphasises the *progressive* aspects of 'individualism', and attempts to specify a *socialist* conception of community which, whilst critical of certain elements of capitalist 'individualism', does not involve any return to the *pre*-individualist social relationships of feudal society, with the correspondingly pre-individualist nature of individual selfhood itself.

These remarks about self-interest, individualism and community are, as I said initially, extremely schematic. They are intended mainly to suggest that an adequate analysis of the place of individual rights in a socialist society – both 'rights of man' and 'rights of the citizen' – must be placed within a much broader historical and normative framework than is usually employed, and to indicate some of the main elements in such a framework.

Before returning to my final evaluation of Kolakowski's thesis of the nascent totalitarianism of Marx's view of the unity of civil and political society, I will make two more remarks about the relevance of these schematic comments on individualism to Marx's attitude towards civil society (Marx 1975). First, alongside his claims about its egoism are others that, roughly speaking, anticipate the charge of 'alienation' developed in the *Paris manuscripts* of the following year, 1844. For instance, he summarises his criticism of the 'rights of man' like this: 'Therefore not one of the so-called rights of man goes beyond egoistic man, man as a member of civil society, namely an individual withdrawn into himself, his private interest and his private desires and separated from the community' (Marx 1975, p. 230). Now, although I cannot argue this here, I think that once we reject a *single* dichotomy between 'individualism' and 'community', this must lead us towards a more dialectical view of the concept of alienation. That is, we should recognise that from one standpoint, the existence of alienated relationships within capitalism reflects certain of its *progressive* features by comparison with feudalism. In particular, as G. A. Cohen has persuasively argued, Marx rightly viewed the alienated character of capitalist labour as having released humans from the bondage of feudal community, in which individual identity was given by reference to people's pre-assigned social positions in the division of labour. Thus alienated labour is to be *transcended* in socialist society – both 'abolished' and 'preserved'.[11]

Second, whatever the implications of Marx's conceptual framework (Marx 1975), it is quite clear that in many of his later writings, such as the *Grundrisse*, he himself made considerable efforts to locate the individualism of capitalist society in an essentially forward-looking framework, which emphasised its considerable virtues in comparison with the 'engulfment' of pre-capitalist social relationships.[12] However, I think also that he never got very far in articulating a concrete conception of socialism that transcended the opposition between feudal community and capitalist individualism: that is, one that both negated and preserved each of the opposing pair. Nor has very much progress been made in doing so since.

5 *Conclusion: socialism's transcendence of liberal rights*

As I noted in my initial account of Kolakowski's view, he seems to regard Marx's ideal of the unity of civil and political society as involving another, perfect unity, that of 'the personal and communal life of every individual', and he argues that attempts to achieve the latter will in fact generate the existence of coercive political bodies, which fail to recognise liberal-democratic political rights. In this way, he claims, Marx's original intention of eliminating the existence of 'separate political bodies' by making political power itself unnecessary, was bound in practice to produce its very opposite.

I share much of Kolakowski's antipathy to the way in which, at least in his early writings, Marx often appears to endorse as an ideal just that 'perfect unity' of the personal and the communal which Kolakowski rejects – though I suspect that I would not share some of his grounds for this rejection, since these seem to involve a more fixed conception of 'human nature', the ineliminability of conflicting interests, than I think plausible: to put it crudely, I would prefer to defend (some aspects of) 'the pursuit of self-interest' on directly normative grounds, than claim this as

[11] Cohen 1974. I have found this a tremendously illuminating piece.

[12] See, e.g., Gould 1978, who bases her very helpful account mainly on the *Grundrisse*.

a part of the human condition. And I have suggested that this harmonistic ideal is implicit in the way Marx (1975) characterises civil society. Further, I argued there that Marx is mistaken in claiming that the 'rights of man', especially the general right to liberty (as distinct from the specific political liberties of the citizen), necessarily presuppose the egoism of civil society.

However, against Kolakowski, I claimed that when we examine Marx's attitude towards 'political emancipation', it emerges that in itself, the ideal of the unity of civil and political society – the overcoming of their separation – does not involve the elimination or redundancy of political rights. Instead, we can see this ideal as requiring the ending of the *abstractness* of citizenship: and this means the extension, and the realisation, of the rights of citizenship throughout the areas of social life previously belonging to the sphere of civil society, whilst also making them more effective in the political sphere itself.

There is, though, at least one major objection to the position I have been proposing, to the extent that it claims to be based upon an accurate exegesis of Marx (1975). As I mentioned in section 2, Marx there says that the very existence of the political state presupposes that of civil society. How then can I claim that 'the unity of civil and political society' can involve maintaining and extending the principles and rights belonging to political society, since these must surely 'disappear' along with civil society, being a presupposition of it?

But I think this objection can be met. First, though, here are two passages where Marx makes this presupposition claim:

> This *man* [i.e. *egoistic* man], the member of civil society, is now the foundation, the presupposition of the *political* state. In the rights of man the state acknowledges him as such. (Marx 1975, p. 233)

And:

> yet the political annulment of private property does not mean the abolition of private property; on the contrary, it even presupposes it . . . the state allows private property, education and occupation to *act* and assert their *particular* nature in *their* own way, i.e. as private property, as education and as occupation. Far from abolishing these *factual* distinctions, the state presupposes them in order to exist, it only experiences itself as *political state* and asserts its *universality* in opposition to these elements. (*ibid.*, p. 219)

Now, a possible reading of these passages (especially the second) which I wish strongly to resist goes like this: Marx is here arguing that the rights and principles of the modern liberal-democratic state presuppose the existence of an economic system based on private property and other such 'distinctions' so that, when that system changes, these rights and principles will become inappropriate, irrelevant or redundant.

This interpretation – associated, of course, with the unfortunately long tradition of supposedly Marxist 'critiques' of liberal democracy as merely the political vehicle for capitalism – seems to me quite mistaken. The alternative reading which I suggest is this. What presupposes the 'distinctions' of civil society is *not* the principles and rights of 'the political state', but the existence of a form of society in which these principles and rights are confined and restricted to the operation of a distinct and limited set of so-called 'political' institutions and practices. In other words, it is the political state *as a separate realm operating with a distinctive conception of human relationships expressed in 'the rights of the citizen'* that presupposes civil society. It is the *abstractness* of the citizenship embodied in the political state, *not* the basic character of the rights and principles of that citizenship, that Marx is here objecting to. It is the state as an especially privileged, distinct realm in which humans, *qua* citizens, are seen as equal participants engaged in communal decisions and relationships, that presupposes civil society – for, were civil society itself to be transformed on the model of political society, the differentiation between political and civil society would no longer exist.

One last comment on Kolakowski's position arises from this. As was noted, he says that Marx's vision of the unity of civil and political society involves the elimination of 'separate political bodies'. Against this, he claims that:

> Societies based on a universal – and still spreading – interdependence of all elements of the technological and economic structures are bound to produce separate bodies both for economic management and for mediating the conflicting aspirations of different sections, and these bodies will in turn always produce their own particular interests and loyalties.
> (Kolakowski 1974, p. 33)

I am inclined to agree with this; but the point I wish to

emphasise is that, on my account of the unity of civil and political society, there is no implication of the kind Kolakowski here criticises. For, with such a unity, there may still be an important role for institutions with 'separate' or distinct *functions*; but they will no longer be 'separate' in the principles and rights they embody. In other words, there is an ambiguity in the idea of 'separate political bodies' here.

Finally, a few comments on the possible implications of my overall analysis of what is meant by overcoming the separation of civil and political society for contemporary socialist theory and practice. First, the simplistic assumptions involved in the concept of 'bourgeois democracy' must be rejected. The critique of capitalist liberal democracies must be conducted, not on the basis of an undialetical negation of its system of liberal rights, but by revealing their abstract character in a capitalist society. That is, a certain form of 'immanent critique' is necessary, in which the failure of those rights to be realised is demonstrated, together with the inevitability of such failure within capitalism. Take, for instance, the recent dismissal of Derek Robinson, shop-steward at British Leyland, for his part-authorship of a pamphlet criticising the management's plan for Leyland's 'survival'. Here we see a straightforward example of how the supposedly sacred right of free speech is refused application outside the realm of 'political society', in that of production. No successful attempt, as far as I know, has ever been made within liberal political theory to provide a coherent rationale for this kind of systematic limitation of liberal rights. This has to be challenged, both theoretically[13] and in collective forms of political action.

At the same time it is essential that, within socialist theory, serious attention is given not merely to the general issue of 'liberal rights in socialist societies', but to the specific institutional forms through which the transcendence of civil and political society can be achieved. Clearly, this involves many questions arising from areas that, as I noted at the outset, have not been touched upon in this paper, such as the problems of the 'transitional phase', and the place of law, and thus *legally*

[13] A good critique of this kind is Skillen 1977, ch. 2.

enforceable rights, in socialist societies.[14] For instance, it may be that alternative, non- or quasi-legal institutional means for the 'enforcement' of rights and the resolution of conflicting rights need to be developed – and not only 'in theory', but through attempts to construct and operate versions of such alternatives within (but also thereby in opposition to) a capitalist system. Without this, the effectiveness of a socialist critique of capitalism is diminished, and the prospective character of a socialist society is rendered seriously deficient.[15]

REFERENCES

Carrillo, S. 1977. *'Eurocommunism' and the state*. London, Lawrence and Wishart.

Cohen, G. A. 1974. Marx's dialectic of labour. *Philosophy and Public Affairs*, 3, pp. 235–61.

Friedman, M. 1962. *Capitalism and freedom*. Chicago University Press.

Fromm, E. 1960. *The fear of freedom*. London, Routledge and Kegan Paul.

Gould, C. 1978. *Marx's social ontology*. London, MIT Press.

Jessop, R. 1978. Capitalism and democracy. In *Power and the state*, ed. G. Littlejohn *et al.*, pp. 10–51. London, Croom Helm.

Kamenka, E. (ed.) 1978. *Law and society*. London, Edward Arnold.

Keat, R. and Miller, D. 1974. Understanding justice. *Political Theory*, 2, pp. 3–31.

Kolakowski, L. 1974. The myth of human self-identity. In *The Socialist idea*, ed. L. Kolakowski and S. Hampshire, pp. 18–35. London, Weidenfeld and Nicholson.

Lenin, V. I. 1963. *The state and revolution*. In *Selected works*, vol. I. Moscow, Foreign Languages Publishing House.

Lukes, S. 1973. *Individualism*. Oxford, Blackwell.

Marx, K. 1968. Critique of the Gotha programme. In *Karl Marx and Frederick Engels: selected works*, pp. 18–37. London, Lawrence and Wishart.

1975. On the Jewish question. In *Karl Marx: early writings*, ed. L. Colletti, pp. 212–41. Harmondsworth, Penguin.

Nisbet, R. 1970. *The sociological tradition*. London, Heinemann.

Pashukanis, E. (ed.) 1978. *Law and Marxism: a general theory*. London, Inklinks.

Rawls, J. 1972. *A theory of justice*. Oxford University Press.

[14] See, e.g., Pashukanis (ed.) 1978 and Kamenka (ed.) 1978.

[15] Much of this paper has emerged from a jointly taught course in political philosophy at the University of Lancaster. I am grateful to many students for discussion, and especially to my colleague Geoff Smith.

Skillen, A. 1977. *Ruling illusions*. Sussex, Harvester Press.
Thompson, E. P. 1980. *Writing by candlelight*. London, Merlin.
Trilling, L. 1972. *Sincerity and authenticity*. London, Oxford University Press.

4 *Does equality destroy liberty?*

RICHARD NORMAN

1 *Diversity*

The enemies of equality have regularly attempted to justify their hostility by claiming that the values of equality and liberty are, in practice if not in principle, antithetical. Human beings, it is argued, differ greatly in their skills and abilities. Inevitably, therefore, some will tend to be more successful than others, and this natural tendency towards inequality can be countered only by the authoritarian suppression of individual talents and aspirations. Hume said it all, with admirable brevity, in 1751:

> Render possessions ever so equal, men's different degrees of art, care, and industry will immediately break that equality . . . The most rigorous inquisition . . . is requisite to watch every inequality on its first appearance; and the most severe jurisdiction, to punish and redress it . . . So much authority must soon degenerate into tyranny.
> (Hume 1751, p. 194)

The thesis has now, apparently, attained the status of official government policy. Here is F. A. Hayek, the intellectual inspiration of our present rulers:

> From the fact that people are very different it follows that, if we treat them equally, the result must be inequality in their actual position, and that the only way to place them in an equal position would be to treat them differently . . . The equality before the law which freedom requires leads to material inequality . . . The desire of making people more alike in their condition cannot be accepted in a free society as a justification for further and discriminatory coercion. (Hayek 1960, p. 87)

Finally let our rulers speak for themselves. Here is Sir Keith Joseph:

> That the pursuit of equality has in practice led to inequality and tyranny . . . is not mere accident. It is the direct result of contradictions which are inherent in the very concept of equality. Egalitarians rely for the achievement of their objects on the coercive power of the State, as they

are bound to do by the nature of the human material with which they deal. A society in which the choices fundamental to human existence are determined by coercion is not a free society. It follows irresistibly that egalitarians must choose between liberty and equality.

(Joseph and Sumption 1979, p. 47)

The anti-egalitarian argument has been regularly mounted; it has been as regularly answered.[1] Nevertheless, as is the way with ideology, it persists despite having been refuted. This may suggest that a further attempt at refutation, such as I am about to undertake, would be a somewhat futile enterprise. But though I accept that the intellectual refutation of ideology can have only a limited effect, it can have *some* good effect. Hence the attempt which follows.

An immediate, and substantially effective, response to the anti-egalitarian argument is to insist on the difference between 'equality' and 'uniformity'.[2] The anti-egalitarian relies heavily on the assumption that equality would require the elimination of all major differences between individuals. Given this assumption, it then seems plausible to maintain that, given the great diversity of people's talents and interests, the required uniformity can be achieved only by a repressive levelling down which prevents such talents from being realised. Some people are, it is said, quite inescapably better than others at playing the violin, at long-distance running, at writing poetry or doing symbolic logic; and these people will inevitably excel, unless they are forcibly prevented from doing so. However, the initial assumption is of course unwarranted. 'Equality' does *not* mean 'uniformity', and an egalitarian society would not be a society in which no one excelled in skilled activities. Rather, it would be a society in which all, in their different ways and with the help of their differing talents, could enjoy an equally worthwhile and satisfying life.[3]

1 Two useful replies are: Tawney 1964, ch. v, section 2 and Carritt 1967.

2 The distinction is excellently made in Bruce Landesman's paper 'Egalitarianism revived' (forthcoming). I should like to acknowledge my debt to this paper, from which I have learned a great deal and which has stimulated my own thinking about the problems discussed in the present paper.

3 The concept of equality as 'equal well-being' which I employ in this paper is taken from Landesman's article cited above. I have also benefited from Nielsen 1979, another valuable discussion of how to formulate this kind of egalitarianism and what its implications are.

This answer, important though it is, will only take us part of the way. The anti-egalitarian is likely to retort that, though differences between people in respect of their talents and achievements may not themselves *constitute* inequalities, they will inevitably tend to *produce* inequalities. The skilled and the talented will be better placed to achieve rewarding lives for themselves. Differences of temperament will have a similar effect. Persons endowed with an energetic disposition, or with an equable temperament, stand to get more out of life than their more sluggish or morose fellows. In short, human capacities for happiness are so multiform that equality in this area can be reached only by massive external intervention in people's lives. 'Equality of well-being' or 'equality of satisfaction' is thus bound to prove an authoritarian ideal.

This case, too, can be answered; but rather than answer it directly, I want at this point to enlarge my ambitions. Liberty and equality, I wish to argue, are not just compatible values, they are interdependent. The ideal of a free society, properly understood, coincides with the ideal of an equal society. And I believe that I can most effectively defend the weaker 'compatibility' thesis by arguing for the stronger 'interdependence' thesis. My defence of the interdependence thesis will involve first examining the concept of liberty, then examining the concept of equality, and thereby revealing the links between them.

2 *Liberty*

It has regularly been recognised that the defence of something like the interdependence thesis tends to appeal to a positive rather than a negative conception of liberty. Accordingly we find the anti-egalitarians frequently insisting on the negative conception, and maintaining that the positive conception of liberty, which is supposed to be more easily linked with equality, is not really a concept of liberty at all, but something else masquerading as liberty. Hayek is a good example of this, and I shall frequently direct my arguments at him in this section. In the first chapter of Hayek's *The constitution of liberty* (1960) we find him saying that though one can indeed use the term 'liberty' or 'freedom' as one wishes, the only sense with which he is concerned is the negative definition of freedom as absence of coercion by other human beings (*ibid.*, pp. 11f). Freedom so defined presupposes, as he says, 'that the individual has some assured private sphere, that there is some set of circumstances in his environment with which others cannot interfere' (*ibid.*, p. 13). Here we have the classical negative picture of liberty – liberty as absence of interference, the non-intrusion by other human beings into what Mill calls 'a circle around every individual human being', 'a space entrenched around', a 'reserved territory'.[4]

There is of course a long history of debate about negative and positive liberty, to which I cannot possibly do justice here.[5] Since it is, however, essential to my argument that I should appeal to the positive rather than the negative conception of liberty, I shall have to say something about how and why I would want to defend it. I shall do this by first acknowledging certain dangers in the positive view, in order then to distinguish what I take to be valid in it.

Consider, then, a characteristic formulation, which I take from Caudwell (1938). The essay contains much which I shall want to endorse: that people do not become free simply by being left alone, that liberty requires certain positive prerequisites, material and social and intellectual. But now consider the following passage:

> Any definition of liberty is humbug that does not mean this: liberty to do what one wants. A people is free whose members have liberty to do what they want – to get the goods they desire and avoid the ills they hate. What do men want? They want to be happy, and not to be starved or despised or deprived of the decencies of life. They want to be secure, and friendly with their fellows, and not conscripted to slaughter and be slaughtered. They want to marry, and beget children, and help, not oppress each other. Who is free who cannot do these things, even if he has a vote, and free speech? Who then is free in bourgeois society, for not a few men but millions are forced by circumstances to be unemployed, and miserable, and despised, and unable to enjoy the decencies of life? (Caudwell 1938, p. 225)

In the light of this, Caudwell goes on to claim that:

> as Russia shows, even in the dictatorship of the proletariat, before the

[4] These phrases are all taken from Mill 1848, bk v, ch. xi, section 2.
[5] The classic discussion is Berlin 1969.

classless State has come into being, man is already freer. He can avoid unemployment, and competition with his fellows, and poverty. He can marry and beget children, and achieve the decencies of life. He is not asked to oppress his fellows. (*ibid*., p. 227)

This was written in the thirties, at the height of the Stalinist autocracy – the period of the purges, the show trials, forced labour, forced collectivisation of agriculture and so on. Bearing this in mind, one can see how the assertion that, despite all this, the people of the Soviet Union were freer, because they were better fed and better housed and therefore had what they wanted, is more than enough to give positive liberty a bad name.

What has gone wrong in the Caudwell passage? Notice first the slide from defining freedom as '*doing* what one wants' to defining it as '*getting*' what one wants. From being a feature of human action, freedom comes to be seen instead as a matter of gaining satisfactions. This is then followed by the assumption that the wants whose satisfaction constitutes freedom are simply fixed and given, that their content can be taken for granted and that the only problem is how to satisfy them. There is no suggestion that people might need to *choose* what it is that they want, and how they want it. And this is what I take to be the crucial thing missing from Caudwell's account of freedom: *the exercise of choice*.

In emphasising the centrality of choice to human freedom, we can do justice to the fact stressed by the 'negative liberty' theorists that freedom does indeed require absence of coercion. If human beings are compelled by others to act in certain ways, they are to that extent unable to exercise their own choice of how to act. Therefore, in so far as people are coerced, they are indeed unfree – and we should not forget this, as Caudwell and others are sometimes inclined to do. However, by stressing the positive fact of choice rather than the mere negative fact of non-interference, we can also do justice to the fact that freedom requires more than mere absence of coercion. People are not enabled to exercise their capacity for choice simply by being left alone. Along these lines, then, we shall be able to see why freedom does indeed depend on positive material and social prerequisites. I shall try to show this in a moment, but before doing so I want to look at two objections to the equating of freedom with the availability of effective choice together with the capacity to exercise it.

The first objection I take from Hayek. He says:

> the range of physical possibilities from which a person can choose at a given moment has no direct relevance to freedom. The rock climber on a difficult pitch who sees only one way out to save his life is unquestionably free, though we would hardly say he has any choice . . . Whether [a person] is free or not does not depend on the range of choice.
>
> (Hayek 1960, p. 12f)

Is the case of the rock climber a counter-example to my proposal? Do we really have here a situation where a person has no choice, but is still free? I want to suggest that the kind of choice we are talking about in this example is a *choice of means*, and that when I propose to define freedom in terms of choice, this should be taken as referring to a *choice of ends*. Hence the example can be accommodated. Given that a person is pursuing certain ends, the fact that he has no choice as to the means he can adopt does not make him less free. It would do so only if some of the actual or possible means also had value as ends in themselves. Only in such a case would the fact that he could not pursue his ends in this way rather than that constitute a restriction on his freedom. A limitation on one's choice of means to a given end is not *ipso facto* a limitation on one's freedom. On the other hand, a limitation on one's choice of ends to pursue *is* a limitation on one's freedom.

A more substantial objection, I think, would be the following. One does not, it might be said, increase a person's freedom simply by increasing the sheer quantity of possibilities which he or she can choose from. Suppose, for example, that I enjoy instant coffee. Suppose that I buy my coffee at a shop which normally stocks two brands of instant coffee. One day I find that the shop has introduced twenty additional brands of instant coffee, all tasting almost the same, 'so as to offer our customers greater freedom of choice'. Here it seems plausible to assert that this merely quantitative increase in the possibilities available has not really increased my freedom. The fact that I now have to choose from twenty-two brands instead of two is simply a drag. It seems to follow, then, that increasing one's range of choice does not necessarily increase one's freedom.

What this example shows, I think, is that we cannot define freedom in purely formal terms. In the example my freedom of choice is not increased, because the additional choices are entirely pointless choices. On the other hand, if there were a total monopoly in coffee, so that only one brand was ever available, or if there were no choice between instant and real coffee, there *would* be less freedom of choice. The conclusion to draw, then, is that the degree of one's freedom depends on the range of *meaningful* or *relevant* choice.

What makes a choice meaningful or relevant? There is no general formal principle to which we can appeal here. In the coffee example, the reason why the choice between real coffee and instant coffee is a relevant choice, but the choice between twenty-two brands is a pointless choice, is that people's tastes in coffee do vary, but not that much. The only way of specifying the range of choice which is necessary for freedom is to say that choice must extend over the normal range of human desires and tastes. In other words, what counts as meaningful freedom is determined by the kinds of things which human beings do as a matter of fact tend to want, and the ways in which they do in fact vary from one another.[6]

This claim gains further support if we think about the standard cases of coercion. What makes a threat coercive? Suppose that I am running a protection racket. I threaten to smash up your betting shop unless you pay protection money. 'Look,' I say, in true Mafia style, 'I'm offering you a choice, what are you complaining about? Either I deprive you of your livelihood, or you pay me the money – it's entirely up to you, you're quite free.' Now obviously what has to be said here is that this is not a real choice. Why not? In reply we can only refer to the importance which people's means of livelihood necessarily have for them. One's means of livelihood is simply not something which one can realistically sacrifice, even though in a sense it is perfectly possible for one to do so. The facts of human nature and the human condition are decisive here and they are, in

[6] My formulation here simplifies what is in fact a very complex issue. Some of the complexities in the relationship between the amount of people's freedom and the range and value of the choices open to them are discussed in G. A. Cohen 1981, especially in the central digression of the paper.

general, what must determine what counts as a realistic or meaningful choice.

Freedom, then, I take to be the availability of, and capacity to exercise, meaningful and effective choice. If this is correct, we can now go on to look at the positive prerequisites of freedom. 'Positive liberty' theorists have regularly linked freedom with the possession of social and institutional powers (such as the political franchise);[7] with material and economic requirements; and with the possession of education and acquisition of knowledge. Power, wealth and education – the relevance of these is not, as the Caudwell passage appears to suggest, that they are things people want, and that in obtaining them they get what they want and are therefore free. The point is rather that they are sources of our capacity to exercise choice. That is to say, they are not just specific *objects* of our choices, they are things that *enable* us to make choices. To the extent that people have access to social power, material wealth and education, they are in a better position to make choices for themselves and therefore enjoy greater freedom. My formulation here obviously entails that I see freedom as something which admits of degrees. The multiple sources of freedom are such that some may be present and not others. I may enjoy a substantial amount of power and material wealth, and to that extent enjoy a degree of freedom, but this freedom may be limited by my ignorance and irrationality and the narrowness of my mental horizons. Or again, I may have certain kinds of social powers but not others. In all such cases I have some freedom, but could have more.

I shall now look briefly at power, wealth and education in turn. In each case I shall try to show their relevance to freedom by looking at Hayek's arguments for dissociating them from his preferred concept of freedom.

(i) *Social and institutional powers*: Hayek contrasts his own use of the term 'freedom' with another use which is

generally recognised as distinct. It is what is commonly called 'political

[7] Hereafter I use the word 'power' to mean *social* power, the power assigned to people by particular social arrangements. This is to be contrasted with the power over nature which takes the form of *technical* mastery of natural processes. In any actual society, of course, the two are closely intertwined, but I cannot in this paper go into the details of the relation between them.

freedom', the participation of men in the choice of their government, in the process of legislation, and in the control of administration. It derives from an application of our concept to groups of men as a whole which gives them a sort of collective liberty. But a free people in this sense is not necessarily a people of free men; nor need one share in this collective freedom to be free as an individual. It can scarcely be contended that the inhabitants of the District of Columbia, or resident aliens in the United States, or persons too young to be entitled to vote do not enjoy full personal liberty because they do not share in political liberty.

(Hayek 1960, p. 13)

There are two confusions here. The first is that Hayek runs together national independence and democratic government. The former is indeed simply the collective analogue of freedom; from the fact that nation A is no longer ruled by nation B, it certainly does not follow that the inhabitants of A are any freer than they were before. Whether they are in fact freer will depend on what kind of political system is then instituted. On the other hand I do want to claim that if a form of democratic politics is then created, the individual members of A *will* have become freer than they were before.

Hayek denies this too. He argues that one may not have the vote, yet still enjoy full personal liberty. Now I certainly agree that one may lack the vote and yet enjoy *some* liberty; in such a situation there are still likely to be some areas of my life over which I do exercise control and in which I act according to my own choices. Therefore one cannot equate liberty *solely* with political power. Nevertheless I also want to say that if I do acquire the power to participate in government or other institutionalised decision-making, I have to that extent *increased* my liberty, I have gained *more* of that freedom which I already to some extent possessed. Previously I exercised *some* control over my life, I had *some* capacity to exercise choices; now, to the extent that I have acquired political power, I have gained *more* of the same kind of freedom, for I have *more* control over my own life, *more* capacity for choice.

It looks otherwise only because Hayek and others regularly focus on that minimal political power which consists in acquiring the right to cast a vote every five years. Certainly gaining that right does not greatly increase my freedom. That, however, is only because it does not greatly increase my political power, and thus does not greatly increase my capacity for choice. Accordingly the example does not undermine the link between political power and freedom, it merely shows that a very little increase in political power can constitute only a very little increase in freedom. Consider an alternative example where there might be a really substantial increase in people's institutional power. Take the case of an economic enterprise placed under workers' control. Assume that it is a case of their being given genuine collective control over the enterprise, not just a case of window-dressing. This would mean that innumerable aspects of their work which they had previously had to accept as given would now be matters for open choice, matters which could be determined by their own intentions and decisions. I take this to constitute a radical increase in their freedom, and to do so just in so far as it is a radical increase in their institutional power.

(ii) *Economic wealth*: Again I take Hayek as my representative opponent. He says:

> This confusion of liberty as power with liberty in its original meaning inevitably leads to the identification of liberty with wealth; and this makes it possible to exploit all the appeal which the word 'liberty' carries in the support for a demand for the redistribution of wealth. Yet, though freedom and wealth are both good things which most of us desire and though we often need both to obtain what we wish, they still remain different. Whether or not I am my own master and can follow my own choice and whether the possibilities from which I must choose are many or few are two entirely different questions. The courtier living in the lap of luxury but at the beck and call of his prince may be much less free than a poor peasant or artisan, less able to live his own life and to choose his own opportunities for usefulness. (*ibid.*, p. 17)

Now if, in this example, the courtier is at the beck and call of his prince, he is indeed to that extent unfree. I am not concerned to identify freedom solely with the possession of economic wealth, and I have allowed that one way in which a person's choices may be limited is through direct coercion by another human being. What we have so far, then, is a comparison between two people who are both unfree, albeit for different reasons. Suppose that we then change the terms of the comparison. Suppose that neither the courtier nor the peasant is at the beck and call of a prince, and that the comparison is simply in respect of the courtier's luxury and the peasant's straitened circumstances. I then do want to say that the courtier has, to that extent, more freedom. In virtue of his wealth, he has many more possibilities for choice open to him. He has much more opportunity to direct his life in accordance with his own desires and intentions, instead of having the pattern of his life largely dictated to him by the narrow limits of the possibilities open to him.

(iii) *Education and knowledge*: The relevance of these to freedom has often been presented as a matter of their contribution to the *effectiveness* of our choices. The more knowledge and understanding we have, it is said, and the more we are able to think rationally and coherently, the more successful we shall be in controlling our environment and in carrying out our wishes and satisfying our desires. This view is, in turn, attacked as confusing liberty with something like 'effective power'. Hayek, for example, says:

> Whether or not a person is able to choose intelligently between alternatives, or to adhere to a resolution he has made, is a problem distinct from whether or not other people will impose their will upon him. (*ibid*., p. 15)

And again:

> It is only too easy to pass from defining liberty as the absence of restraint to defining it as the 'absence of obstacles to the realization of our desires', or even more generally as 'the absence of external impediment'. This is equivalent to interpreting it as effective power to do whatever we want. (*ibid*., p. 17)

Whatever may be said about this link between understanding and the *effectiveness* of our choices, there is a more fundamental link: between the capacity for rational understanding and the *capacity to make choices at all*. The ability to make choices is not an innate capacity, present in the new-born child. It develops only with the growth of understanding. The new-born child cannot be said to make choices, because it has no awareness of possibilities. Its behaviour is purely a response to immediate stimuli, and only gradually does it become capable of making free choices as it acquires the ability to envisage desirable alternatives which are not immediately at hand and which contrast with the existing state of affairs. This capacity to envisage alternatives is increased enormously by the acquisition of language. The process is not, however, one which has any natural terminus. As we acquire education and experience, we thereby come to understand our world and are increasingly able to conceive of alternatives to the present situation, and to think rationally about ways of realising alternatives. If that sounds a rather mundane ability, think of Herbert Marcuse's account of 'one-dimensional man' who equates the given world with the only possible world (Marcuse 1964). However exaggerated and incomplete Marcuse's account may be, there can be no doubt about the role which ideology plays in limiting people's awareness of the choices which are objectively open to them. The pushing back of these restraints is the enlargement of freedom.

I am claiming, then, that political and institutional power, economic wealth and the growth of understanding through education and experience, are positive sources of freedom, and that the absence of these is as much an impediment to freedom as is direct coercion. To complete this claim I want finally to consider a general objection to it, which would run as follows. However important these sources of freedom may be, there is a crucial difference between them and the absence of coercion. The difference is that between human and non-human restraints on action. If I am coerced, I am prevented from acting by other human beings. If I lack social power, or wealth or education, it is not other human beings who prevent me acting in certain ways. The difference between the two is fundamental, and the best way of marking it is to reserve the word 'freedom' for only one of the two. Thus Hayek says that 'freedom', in his preferred sense, 'refers solely to a relation of men to other men' (Hayek 1960, p. 12).

Well, there does seem to be *some* kind of difference here, and whether we want the word 'freedom' to straddle the distinction, or be confined to one side of it, may seem at first to be merely a matter for stipulative definition. Suppose, however, that we go on to ask why this difference should be so important. It is likely to be said that if restraints are imposed by human beings, then human action can remove them, whereas if they are not so imposed, they cannot be removed in that way. But is it so simple? There are surely impediments to freedom, other than direct coercion, which can be removed or altered by human action, and the ones which we are considering – lack of social power, or wealth or education – all fall into that category. The distribution of each of these things can be changed by human action.

As an illustration of how the distinction begins to shift, consider Isaiah Berlin's treatment of it. He begins with what looks like a firm demarcation:

> Coercion implies the deliberate interference of other human beings with the area in which I could otherwise act. You lack political liberty or freedom only if you are prevented from attaining a goal by human beings. (Berlin 1969, p. 122)

There we have the same tight restriction on the use of the word 'freedom' which we find with Hayek. But Berlin continues:

> If my poverty were a kind of disease, which prevented me from buying bread, or paying for a journey round the world, or getting my case heard [in the law courts], as lameness prevents me from running, this inability would not naturally be described as a lack of freedom, least of all political freedom. It is only because I believe that my inability to get a given thing is due to the fact that other human beings have made arrangements whereby I am, whereas others are not, prevented from having enough money with which to pay for it, that I think myself a victim of coercion or slavery . . . The criterion of oppression is the part that I believe to be played by other human beings, directly or indirectly, with or without the intention of doing so, in frustrating my wishes. (*ibid.*)

This is a much looser claim. Berlin is not now saying that I am unfree only if I am directly and deliberately coerced by others. He is saying that I am unfree if my choices are limited by social arrangements attributable to, or alterable by, human agency. And once one makes this concession (as I think Berlin is right to do), a great deal more has to be admitted. Even his example of lameness becomes contentious. Whether my lameness can be cured, and how drastically it will inhibit my activities, will depend very much on the adequacy of the health care facilities available to me in my society, and that is something which is determined by human agency. Thus the dividing line between natural and human impediments leaves a great deal more on the human side of the line than might at first appear. Certainly the things which I have been stressing – access to social power, to economic wealth and to education – come under the heading of social arrangements made by human beings.

I do not think, then, that the confining of 'freedom' to 'absence of coercion' can be justified by arguing that the latter alone is achievable by human agency. To this I would add a positive argument for extending the concept of 'freedom' in the way in which I have been trying to do, and this positive argument is simply an appeal to experience. The appeal to experience tends to be deployed by the critics of 'positive liberty'. They are inclined to say that however much an authoritarian regime may claim that its subjects are better fed or better educated, passing this off as 'freedom' is a sleight of hand which will deceive no one; its subjects know that what they are experiencing, however valuable it may be, is not freedom.

I want to suggest that the test of experience can take us the other way. Of course feeling well-fed is not the same as feeling free. Think however of what an increase in economic well-being may bring with it. Think of someone who unexpectedly inherits a fortune, and becomes aware of entirely new ways of life which are now available. Or in the case of social power, think of the experience of the oppressed who rebel against their intolerable condition, find all resistance crumble and discover that power has fallen into their hands. Or in the case of education, think of someone who, in middle age and after living within fairly limited horizons, decides to go to college and thereby discovers the possibility of entirely new attitudes to life, the possibility of questioning innumerable things which he or she had previously taken for granted. In all these cases I think one can speak quite appropriately of a sense of liberation. By this I mean an awareness of an array of choices which were hitherto quite unavailable or unrecognised. I mean a heady sense of new vistas opening up. I mean the characteristic combination of an exhilarating sense of new possibilities and an awesome feeling of new responsibilities. All of this, experientially, is of a piece with the removal of coercion, as for example in the case of release from prison. The acquisition of power, of wealth and of education *are* experienced as liberation.

3 *Equality*

I turn now to the connection with equality. I said earlier that the egalitarian is concerned not to make everyone alike, but that everyone should have an equally worthwhile and satisfying life. I noted, however, the objection that individual idiosyncrasies, the variety of individual abilities and temperaments would make this very difficult to achieve, and would in practice, even if not in principle, require massive regimentation of people's lives. I now want to propose that though this ideal of 'equal well-being' may be the underlying ethical principle of egalitarianism, it is not what egalitarians have in practice directly aimed at. Rather, they have aimed at creating the *social conditions* which would *enable* people to enjoy equally worthwhile lives. There can be no guarantee that everyone will in fact achieve equal well-being, and indeed the expectation must be that this will never entirely happen, but what we can do is create the kind of society in which there will be no impediments to equal well-being, other than the accidents and vagaries of individual temperaments and inclinations.

What then are these social conditions which egalitarians have in practice been concerned to create? I want to suggest that egalitarians have been concerned above all with the three factors which I have just been discussing: social power, wealth and education. We thus come to the crux of my argument. Egalitarians have in practice aimed at equality of social power, equality of wealth and equality in education – and in the light of the previous section I can then claim that, in these various ways, what egalitarians are aiming at is equality of liberty.

As in the previous section, I shall deal briefly with each of the three factors in turn, and sketch their relevance to equality.

(i) *Equality of social power*: It is an obvious feature of egalitarian writing that it has been concerned not with unequal relations between mere individuals as such, not with the random fact that this person and that person happen to be unequal in some respect, but with unequal relations between social groups. Inequalities between rich and poor, between ruling class and oppressed class, between men and women, between white and black – these are the constant theme. The concern is therefore with the *structural* features of a society, with institutionalised or semi-institutionalised social relations. By 'institutionalised' relations I mean relations embodied in explicit formal rules; by 'semi-institutionalised' I mean those depending on habitualised implicit assumptions which, in conjunction with institutionalised rules, govern the relations between groups. An example of the first would be racial inequality in the South African system of apartheid. An example of the second would be racialism in the United States of the kind which the civil rights movement set out to eliminate. This was not, on the whole, embodied in formal rules securing powers and privileges for whites, it was more a matter of the informal monopolisation of power by whites, grounded in attitudes and prejudices. Notice however that such cases are not *simply* a matter of prejudice. Prejudice creates inequalities only when it is superimposed on relations which *are* institutionalised – on institutions of political power, professional hierarchies, etc.

As an example of egalitarianism which focuses on power relations between social groups, consider the case of Marxism. Marxism has often been thought of as a major instance of egalitarian theory.[8] In fact, however, the classical Marxist writers very rarely invoke the idea of equality, and when they do, their typical attitude is that epitomised by Engels: '. . . the real content of the proletarian demand for equality is the demand for the *abolition of classes*. Any demand for equality which goes beyond that, of necessity passes into absurdity' (Engels 1969, p. 128). Engels's position seems to me to be too narrow (although he is sensitive to other kinds of inequality e.g. between men and women: *The origin of the family, private property and the state*). Class inequality is not the only kind of inequality. As I have already indicated, such things as sexual inequality and racial inequality are distinct from class inequality, and independently important.[9] That is not to imply that they are insulated from one

[8] We have it on no less an authority than that of Sir Keith Joseph that Marxism 'is the only internally coherent egalitarian philosophy': Joseph and Sumption 1979, p. 8.

[9] In fairness to Engels I should acknowledge that in the passage which I have quoted he regards the abolition of classes as 'the real content' of 'the *proletarian* demand for equality'. This is consistent with the view that the demand for equality, when made by other oppressed groups, can properly have a different real content.

another. In recent years Marxists, socialist feminists and others have rightly been concerned with the ways in which these different structures of inequality interact and reinforce each other. But what I mean is this. Socialism, as I understand it, is a movement to destroy class oppression *because it is oppression*. The ethical impulse of socialism is an appeal to a *general* ethics of equality. On that same ethical basis, sexual oppression and racial oppression stand condemned in their own right, because they too are inequalities. Marxists have sometimes given the impression that the only thing wrong with racism is that it divides the working class and so perpetuates class oppression. It does do that, but that is not the only thing wrong with it.

It is, then, a mistake to confine the legitimate application of the concept of equality to the struggle for a classless society. What I do want to agree with, however, is the emphasis on inequality of structural power relations. In the case of class inequality, these power relations are the relations of production. They are ownership relations, the relations which separate the class which owns the means of production and the class which, within the sphere of production, owns only its labour-power. These relations of production give the one class a pervasive power over the other, not just in economic life, but in the making of decisions about the life of the society as a whole. In contrast, socialist, egalitarian relations of production would consist in the common ownership and popular control of the means of production. These would give working people power over their own lives, and especially over their working lives. They would constitute a society in which all would share equally in the making of decisions and choices about the organisation and direction of economic activity, in place of a society in which most people have these choices and decisions made for them. They would, to that extent, constitute the equalisation of freedom, and so would any other social relations which equalised power between different groups.[10]

[10] It might be thought that the phrase 'equality of power' is something of a misnomer, on the grounds that genuinely equal relations between people would do away with power altogether. Certainly the phrase is misleading if it suggests a picture of power as a commodity which can simply be distributed in different proportions, and which retains the same character however it is distributed.

(ii) *Equality of wealth*: It is a difficult question whether inequality of wealth is ultimately reducible to inequality of power. It may help if we distinguish between wealth as means of *production* and wealth as means of *consumption*. If we are talking about the former, that is, about the ownership of wealth as capital, then we *are* talking about inequality of power in the sphere of production. If we then turn to consider wealth under the aspect of consumption, it is in the first place clear that inequalities in consumer wealth follow directly from inequalities in the relations of production. Those who enjoy the greatest material benefits do so because they exercise control over the means of production. Nevertheless we can envisage the possibility of unequal wealth *not* stemming from unequal power. We can, for example, envisage the possibility of a socialist economy with egalitarian relations of production in which, by common agreement, some are given much greater material rewards than others. We might imagine this being agreed to as a consequence of a residual exaggerated respect for certain kinds of human qualities, for example mental rather than manual skills. In this situation, then, equality of power would co-exist with inequality of wealth.

Thoroughgoing egalitarians would, I think, rightly regard this inequality of wealth as objectionable. They would, moreover, see it as important for the reasons I have already indicated. Such inequalities of wealth would make it more difficult for some than for others to enjoy a worthwhile life. Conversely, though individual differences between people make it unpractical and undesirable to try to guarantee that everyone lives an equally worthwhile life, equality of wealth would put everyone equally in a position to live such a life, while leaving them free to utilise the opportunities in whatever ways they see fit.

Equal relations would differ not just quantitatively but qualitatively from relations in which one group or person had power over another. The attempt to create equal relations between men and women, for example, would be an attempt to create relations no longer characterised by domination and submission. Nevertheless, in hanging on to the idea that these equal relations would still be 'power relations', we can mark the fact that any social relations other than the most transitory have to incorporate at least a semi-formalised recognition of how decisions are to be made and who is to make them. (On this point I am grateful for discussions with Vic Seidler and Tony Skillen among others.)

I have deliberately been leaving open the question whether 'wealth' is to be understood as meaning 'money' or 'material goods'. There is a strand in socialist thought which seems to envisage the eventual abolition of money. This might seem to be encouraged by a passage in the 'Critique of the Gotha programme' where Marx suggests that true equality would be attainable only when there had been achieved an economic condition of sheer abundance (Marx and Engels 1962, p. 24).[11] I would accept that economic equality cannot mean *simply* equality of *monetary* wealth. As is stressed in the Marx passage, needs differ. An obvious case would be that of health care. A person suffering from a serious physical disability needs much greater health care than a fit and healthy person. Consequently, if they are equal simply in respect of monetary income, and if the first person has to spend the greater part of his resources on expensive medical treatment, the upshot will be very great inequality in their overall condition. Such examples suggest that an appropriate egalitarian principle would be one of free provision for basic needs. As well as health care these basic needs might include, say, housing, basic foodstuffs and education. I cannot however imagine that *all* needs and desires could be met on this principle of free provision. Marx's vision of total abundance smacks too much of nineteenth-century optimism. There are inescapable limits to what can be produced, there must be inescapable decisions about using limited resources for this purpose rather than that, and therefore in any society there will be relative scarcity in at least some respects. One cannot realistically imagine a situation where people, whether individually or collectively, simply go and help themselves to a rare wine or an artistic masterpiece or an exquisitely carved piece of furniture whenever they feel like it.[12] Accordingly it seems to me

[11] For further references, see Moore 1980. Moore's book is very relevant to the present discussion. He argues that what Marx calls the 'higher phase of communist society', involving the abolition of money and exchange, is never shown by him to be either feasible or desirable, and that it is in fact incompatible with his historical materialism.

[12] It may be objected that I am here assuming the persistence of an individualistic consumer mentality, and ignoring the changes in human desires and attitudes which Marx relies on. (Keith Graham has put this point to me.) I am sure that Marx does presuppose a transformation of human consciousness,

that the feasible alternatives are either that the inevitably limited supply of material goods is shared out between people in predetermined proportions, which would leave very little scope for personal choice, or that there is some kind of monetary system which allows people to choose their material goods in accordance with personal preference. I am here accepting the view, sometimes erroneously thought to be an anti-socialist one, that the existence of money is in practice a necessary condition of effective freedom, and that money would continue to play an important role in an economy which respected the requirements of freedom and equality. A comprehensive egalitarian principle might therefore look something like this: satisfaction of the basic needs of all, plus equality of monetary incomes over and above that (though this might need further qualifying if it were desired to increase some incomes to compensate for particularly unpleasant or dangerous work).

The retention of money may seem incompatible with socialism in so far as the latter involves the abolition of an economy dominated by the commodity form. I do not think that it is. Changing economic production so that it is no longer dominated by the commodity form does not require that one should eliminate money, and commodities, as such. Rather, it is a matter of subordinating exchange to use instead of vice versa. It is possible to produce for need instead of for profit, while still retaining some kind of market system for the distribution of some goods.

(iii) *Equality in education*: Egalitarians have always been much preoccupied with education. It is important to see what the proper reasons for this would be. A slogan often appealed to in this area is 'equality of opportunity'. It has been pointed out that this slogan, as it is applied to education, may quickly cease to be at all egalitarian. If it is applied against the background of a competitive and hierarchical system, it means simply that every-

and to some extent I think that he is right to do so. But, however strong the obsession with individual ownership of consumer goods may be in our own society I think it would be a mistake to suppose that problems of the distribution of goods would simply disappear in a different kind of society; it seems prudent to assume that resources will continue to be limited relative to people's wants, and to take seriously the questions of distribution which then arise.

one has the opportunity to compete, according to his or her ability, for educational rewards and for the economic rewards which may come in their wake. In other words, it means equal opportunity to be unequal.

The proper conclusion to draw from this is not that the principle of equal opportunity is useless, but that it is useless until we answer the question: 'opportunity to do what?' If it means 'opportunity to compete in a hierarchical system', then it is not a substantially egalitarian principle. The genuinely egalitarian use of it, however, would mean 'equal opportunity to live a worthwhile life'. In other words, it would mark precisely that qualification which has, in practice, to be added to the idea of equal well-being. As I have suggested previously, one cannot guarantee that everyone has an equally worthwhile life, but one can arrange social conditions so that everyone has an equal *opportunity* to live a worthwhile life. It is this interpretation of equality, I have been arguing, which amounts to equality of liberty.

Thus understood, equality of opportunity would require the equality of social power and the equality of wealth which I have been discussing. The relevance of education is that it too would be one of the most important *opportunities* – one of the most crucial things possession of which, like possession of social power and of wealth, enables people to live worthwhile lives in accordance with their own choices and preferences. Equal educational opportunity now comes to mean not equal opportunity to compete for education, but equal provision of the kind of education which gives everyone the opportunity to live a worthwhile life. There is no room here to discuss at length what this would mean in practice. Clearly, however, it would require that educational resources should not be concentrated on those with certain particular intellectual skills, but spread evenly among all the different kinds of education which people need, and among all those who need them.[13]

[13] For an indication of the sort of approach I have in mind, see Williams 1965, pt two, ch. 1.

As in the case of wealth, 'equality' in educational resources would have to recognise differences in people's needs. It might require that some people (suffering perhaps from particular physical or mental handicaps) be given special provision in the light of their special or greater needs.

I should add that equality in the provision of education cannot by itself secure equality of opportunity to live a worthwhile life.[14] It cannot possibly do so in a society where there are great inequalities of power and wealth. It is nevertheless important in its own right. It is important especially because, as I argued earlier, education is one of the crucial preconditions enabling people freely to choose for themselves how they are to live.

I have discussed equality of power, equality of wealth and equality of educational provision. There remains one other kind of equality to which egalitarians are commonly thought to be committed: equality of prestige.[15] Of this I would simply say that if we can obtain the other kinds of equality, egalitarians should be quite content to accept inequalities of prestige. Anti-egalitarians are right in this, that a society in which no one ever excelled, in which no one was ever especially looked up to or admired, in which no one ever stood out as an exceptionally accomplished poet or musician or athlete or thinker, would be an intolerable society. On the other hand, it is not clear to me that egalitarians have ever thought otherwise.[16] Prestige is objectionable, and has been objected to, only when it carries power or wealth with it, or accompanies power or wealth.[17]

[14] That it can do so is the sort of claim which tended to be made by some of the more optimistic advocates of comprehensive schooling twenty or so years ago.

[15] Lucas attributes to egalitarians a preoccupation with inequalities of power, prestige and wealth.

[16] Rousseau, in his *Discourse on the origin of inequality*, describes moral or political inequality as consisting of 'the different privileges which some men enjoy to the prejudice of others; such as that of being more rich, more honoured, more powerful, or even in a position to exact obedience': Rousseau 1973, p. 44; cf. also p. 100. This may seem to give the same weight to inequalities of prestige as to those of wealth and power. It is however an open question how important he took inequality of prestige to be. He describes it as emerging in the early stages of human society, when: 'Each one began to consider the rest, and to wish to be considered in turn; and thus a value came to be attached to public esteem. Whoever sang or danced best, whoever was the handsomest, the strongest, the most dexterous, or the most eloquent, came to be of most consideration; and this was the first step towards inequality, and at the same time towards vice' (p. 81). My own reading of Rousseau would be that this 'first step towards inequality' does not become entrenched as social inequality in the full sense until private property has come into being. (On this point I disagree with, but have learnt much from, my colleague Chris Cherry.)

[17] This may be too simple. Differences in prestige may consist not just in some people being admired more than others, but in some people's self-esteem being

4 *A free society*

I have argued that power, wealth and education are basic sources of liberty; that the most important equalities to which egalitarians are committed are equality of power, of wealth and of educational provision; and that to that extent they are concerned to equalise liberties. If the argument is correct, does it establish the interdependence of liberty and equality? It might be objected that even if it shows that egalitarians are committed to equalising liberty, that is not enough; for in *equalising* liberty, they might also *diminish* liberty. Thus a society in which there were equality of liberty might still not be 'a free society'. The question is: what could this mean? I shall consider three possibilities.

(i) Our objector might invoke the traditional liberal picture, of a circle around each individual, circumscribing a sacred territory which must not be violated. It might be said that we equalise power, wealth and education only at the cost of making this territory too small, or too often invaded. I have already said something about the inadequacy of this picture. Human beings do not become free simply by being left alone, and the individualism which the picture encourages may be just what stops people from combining to acquire power over their own lives. Again, there are familiar problems about how one could possibly determine where this supposed line is to be drawn; Mill's proposal, that it should be drawn between self-regarding and other-regarding actions, notoriously fails to do justice to the social character of all human actions. We might ask, too, what is supposed to be the source of this external interference in the lives of individuals. The standard answer is: government, the state. But if we are envisaging equal distribution of power, this will mean that political power is no longer monopolised by institutions standing over against individuals; the external source of interference disappears.

fundamentally threatened. The prevailing customs of a society may, for instance, require that certain groups constantly humiliate themselves in relation to others. I am inclined to think that in any actual society such practices would accompany inequalities of power and wealth, as ideological means of sustaining and legitimising those inequalities. Nevertheless the one could conceivably exist without the other, and would then constitute a separate problem.

What does remain a real possibility is that, as the collective holders of shared power, people might impose excessively on certain of their own number, considered as the holders of individual aims and aspirations. In other words, something like Mill's 'tyranny of the majority ' would still be possible, and in this respect the equalities we have been considering would *in principle* be *compatible* with excessive coercion. Whether those equalities would *in practice* be likely to *increase* coercion is another matter. What seems much more plausible is the traditional democratic claim that equality of power is a better safeguard than inequality of power against excessive coercion.

(ii) It might be said that in creating the equalities we have been considering, one would be decreasing the liberty of *some* people, namely those who formerly possessed a greater share of powers and privileges. This of course is true. In equalising liberty, you increase the liberty of some only by decreasing the liberty of others. There may be some sense in which greater equality increases the freedom of all. Such a case could, I think, be argued.[18] But there remain other and more obvious senses in which equality diminishes some people's freedom.

I do not think, however, that this is a fact to which anti-egalitarians such as Hayek and his followers could readily appeal. However prepared they may be to assert the inescapability of elites, and to defend the economic and cultural privileges of elites, they certainly do not want to treat freedom as an elite privilege. They see themselves as defending not the freedom of certain groups, but 'a free society'. They cannot, therefore, claim that this 'free society' is threatened when the freedom of only a privileged section is diminished. So the question remains what sense can be given to this idea of a free society other than as meaning a society of *equal* freedom.

(iii) One other possibility would be to appeal to something like Rawls's 'Difference Principle' in the matter of freedom

[18] The most plausible version of such a thesis would, I think, be the Marxist claim that only when economic processes are brought under collectively shared human control do they cease to be alien forces dominating human beings, and become subject to human choices. When some people dominate others in the 'free' market, all are dominated by the market. See Marx and Engels 1970, pp. 54–5 and 83–6; Engels, Socialism Utopian and scientific in Marx and Engels 1962, p. 153; Caudwell 1938, pp. 223–5.

(Rawls 1972). It could be argued that departures from the equalities we have been considering would produce a freer society because they would increase the freedom even of the least free; and that they would do so because inequalities of power, wealth and educational resources would produce, even for the least advantaged, *more* power, wealth and educational resources.

Could this plausibly be maintained? Certainly not in the case of power, which I have been presenting as the most fundamental equality. Power, at any rate in the sense in which I have been considering it, is essentially a relation between persons. If some people have more power than others, they necessarily have it at the *expense* of others, because it is power *over* those others. Therefore it would be contradictory to suppose that by distributing power unequally we could increase the power of the least powerful.

However, an analogous argument could be and has been maintained in the case of wealth. It is claimed that if we accord greater power to an elite, if we lavish educational resources upon them in their youth, and ply them with economic incentives when they have been educated, their technocratic skills will produce an abundance of wealth for even the least privileged of us. In increasing the wealth available for all of us, they would also be increasing the resources which could be devoted to the education of all of us. Therefore, accepting my claim that wealth and educational resources are essential components of freedom, it could in this way be argued that such inequalities would increase the freedom even of the least advantaged.

This thesis is indeed a possible one. That is to say it is not philosophically incoherent. But if we consult experience, there is no reason to think that it is true. It has a limited truth, perhaps, within a certain kind of society. Given the motivational structures which a capitalist economy fosters and sustains, it may be true that the functioning of such an economy requires hierarchical structures and incentives. This however is only a statement about the inevitable character of capitalism. It does not follow that any human society can achieve material prosperity only by offering radically unequal rewards. In view of the demoralising effects of inequality, the general level of wealth is much more likely to be maximised through the energies and commitments which would be promoted by equal sharing in a common enterprise.

I have considered three respects in which it might be maintained that a more equal society would be a less free society. I have suggested that none of the three claims is convincing. It is more plausible to suppose that a free society would be one in which liberty is equally shared by all. I conclude that the struggle for equality is not just compatible with, but coincides with, the struggle for a free society.[19]

REFERENCES

Berlin, I. 1969. Two concepts of liberty. In *Four essays on liberty*. London, Oxford University Press.

Carritt, E. F. 1967. Liberty and equality. In *Political philosophy*, ed. A. Quinton, pp. 127–40. Oxford University Press.

Caudwell, C. 1938. *Studies in a dying culture*. London, Bodley Head.

Cohen, G. A. 1981. Illusions about private property and freedom. In *Issues in Marxist philosophy*, vol. IV, ed. J. Mepham and D.-H. Ruben. Sussex, Harvester Press.

Engels, F. 1969. *Anti-Dühring*. Moscow, Foreign Languages Publishing House.

Hayek, F. A. 1960. *The constitution of liberty*. London, Routledge and Kegan Paul.

Hume, D. 1751. *An enquiry concerning the principles of morals*. In *Hume's Enquiries*, ed. L. A. Selby-Bigge. 1888. Oxford, Clarendon Press.

Joseph, K. and Sumption, J. 1979. *Equality*. London, John Murray.

Lucas, J. R. 1965. Against equality. *Philosophy*, 40, pp. 296–307.

Marcuse, H. 1964. *One-dimensional man*. London, Routledge and Kegan Paul.

Marx, K. and Engels, F. 1962. *Selected works*, vol. II. Moscow, Foreign Languages Publishing House.

1970. *The German ideology*, ed. C. J. Arthur. London, Lawrence and Wishart.

Mill, J. S. 1848. *Principles of political economy*. In *The collected works of John Stuart Mill*. 1963. London, Routledge and Kegan Paul.

[19] This paper has benefited at various points from discussions with and comments from other people, and from other people's work in the area. I should like to thank especially Martin Barker, Larry Blum, Chris Cherry, Jerry Cohen, Keith Graham, Teddi Kachi, Yukio Kachi, Bruce Landesman, Jeff Luttrell, Kai Nielsen, Sean Sayers, Vic Seidler, Tony Skillen and the publishers' anonymous reader.

Moore, S. 1980. *Marx on the choice between socialism and communism*. London, Harvard University Press.
Nielsen, K. 1979. Radical egalitarian justice: justice as equality. *Social Theory and Practice*, 5, pp. 209–26.
Rawls, J. 1972. *A theory of justice*. Oxford University Press.
Rousseau, J-J. 1973. *Discourse on the origin of inequality*. London, Everyman.
Tawney, R. H. 1964. *Equality*. London, Allen and Unwin.
Williams, R. 1965. *The long revolution*. Harmondsworth, Penguin.

PART III

Human Organisation

5 Democracy and the autonomous moral agent

KEITH GRAHAM

Can a rational moral agent accept democratic decisions? In his *In defense of anarchism* (1970)[1] Robert Paul Wolff argued that he could not, and although a considerable literature has accumulated in criticism of Wolff's arguments he has stuck to his guns. Indeed, he now thinks his position is even stronger than he originally claimed (Wolff 1976, p. 84; cf. Wolff 1973, p. 303). I do not think that Wolff's position is in the end a tenable one, but neither do I think his critics have been successful in establishing why it is not. Accordingly, one of my aims in this paper is to defend a recognisably Wolffian position against what may be thought to be some fairly easy refutations. This will entail a certain amount of reconstruction of Wolff's argument which I hope can be seen to be clearly within the spirit of the original. I then attempt to show that Wolff's premises, concerning the supreme importance of the autonomy of moral agents, are not merely compatible with one form of democratic decision-making but actually require it.

In section 1, I summarise Wolff's arguments to the conclusion that there is no justification for obedience to the state. In section 2, I outline a series of objections which seek to show that Wolff's arguments are directed against a man of straw and that individual autonomy is compatible with state authority. In section 3, I suggest that these objections fail, and in section 4, I consider the significance of the cases where Wolff appears to abandon his general position concerning the supreme importance of autonomy. In section 5, I draw out some of the implications of Wolff's own position and attempt to show that it commits him to an acceptance of majoritarianism. In concluding

[1] Wolff's *In defense of anarchism* was reprinted in 1976 with an additional section 'A reply to Reiman', a rejoinder to Reiman 1972. I refer to the main text of Wolff's book as Wolff 1970 and to the additional section as Wolff 1976.

section 6, I relate the results of the argument to the question of the appropriate political stance which they suggest for the real world.

1

Wolff's argument can be set out fairly briefly. He is concerned with the question whether any state has *de jure* authority, the right (as opposed merely to the power) to command its citizens, and whether they have any obligation to obey the commands of such a state. Obedience, he stresses, is not just a matter of doing as you are ordered, or even of doing as you are ordered because you think it is right to act in that way. For you might consider, on independent grounds, that you had an obligation so to act whether anyone had ordered you or not. Rather, obedience is doing what someone tells you to do *because they tell you to* (Wolff 1970, p. 9).

Wolff's view is that there can be no state whose citizens have an obligation of this kind, and he bases his view on a particular conception of the requirements of moral agency. Indeed, he notes in his Preface that he has 'simply taken for granted an entire ethical theory' (*ibid.*, p. viii). It is, he suggests, the first assumption of moral philosophy that people are responsible for their actions: in some sense they are capable of choosing and initiating one course of action rather than another. Moreover, they are able to do so on the basis of *reasoning* – reflecting, deliberating, weighing this consideration against that and so on. For Wolff, this gives rise to an obligation to *take* responsibility for their actions and in doing so to judge for themselves how to behave (*ibid.*, pp. 12–13). I may listen to the advice of others, but must decide for myself whether it is good advice (*ibid.*, p. 13). I may do what someone else tells me to, but not *because* they tell me to (*ibid.*, p. 14). 'Taking responsibility for one's actions means making the final decisions about what one should do' (*ibid.*, p. 15), and that is what the moral agent's autonomy consists in.

Two further points which Wolff makes about moral autonomy should be mentioned: their significance will become apparent later. First, an agent can easily forfeit autonomy, by deciding to obey someone's commands *without* attempting to judge for himself whether they are good (*ibid.*, p. 14); but secondly, Wolff insists that such forfeiture be kept to a minimum: 'The moral condition demands that we acknowledge responsibility and achieve autonomy wherever and whenever possible' (*ibid.*, p. 17). Moral autonomy, then, is not something inescapable, but it is something to be maximised.

The initial conflict between autonomy and state authority now emerges. To the extent that people insist on remaining the authors of their own practical decisions they must resist the suggestion that the state – or indeed any other collective of people – has the right to take those decisions for them, or to tell them what to do. A person may act in accordance with the law if he judges that to be the correct way to behave, but 'he will deny that he has a duty to obey the laws of the state *simply because they are the laws*' (*ibid.*, p. 18).

That is the conflict baldly stated. The next question is whether it disappears when the state in question is a democratic one. Is there, as many would surely wish to claim, something distinctive about a democracy which places a special obligation on its citizens to obey the law and resolves the apparent conflict between autonomy and authority? In answering this, Wolff considers three models of democratic organisation: *unanimous direct democracy*, *representative democracy* and *majoritarianism*.

Originally, Wolff had regarded *unanimous direct democracy* as a genuine solution to his problem (*ibid.*, p. 27), though he subsequently withdrew this (Wolff 1976, p. 88). The distinctive feature of this model is that it is 'a political community in which every person votes on every issue – governed by a rule of unanimity', so that every member 'wills freely every law which is actually passed' (Wolff 1970, p. 23). Hence, Wolff had held that if everyone, including me, agrees to some principles of compulsory arbitration for settling disputes, then in a subsequent operation of them I become bound by the results of arbitration *whatever they are* since they issue from my will (*ibid.*, pp. 24–5).

So why not stop the argument here? Because the specification of the first model is taken to be unrealistic. As soon as any disagreement arises in a community, even in the form of one dissenter, unanimity is lost; and there is in any case the problem of giving all people a vote on every issue in large communities. The second and third models are designed to cope with these two problems.

In *representative democracy* the whole populace is not directly involved in the making of every decision. They elect representatives, perhaps on some general platform, and to that extent the representatives decide on legislation independently of their electors. But to that extent, equally, Wolff argues, the model embodies the original conflict. If I am one of the electors in this model I may like the legislation enacted, I may approve of it and it may serve my interests, but in the circumstances envisaged, where the representatives enact it without any specific mandate from me, it is not an expression of my will (*ibid.*, p. 29). After all, exactly the same might be true of a benevolent dictatorship, and this would evidently fall foul of the requirements of autonomy (*ibid.*, p. 30).

Majoritarianism is intended to cope with the implausibility of maintaining unanimity in any sizeable community, and in this model decisions are enacted provided they attract the support of a majority. Wolff considers a number of arguments in favour of this model, including a cluster of moral and prudential arguments to the effect that majority rule reduces social friction, or advances the general welfare or gives each individual the best chance of advancing his or her own interests (*ibid.*, pp. 39–40). His response is that arguments of this kind are simply irrelevant to the problem of autonomy which he has outlined:

> As justifications for an individual's autonomous decision to cooperate with the state, they may be perfectly adequate; but as demonstrations of the *authority* of the state – as proofs, that is, of the right of the state to command the individual and of his obligation to obey, *whatever may be commanded* – they fail completely. If the individual retains his autonomy by reserving to himself in each instance the final decision whether to cooperate, he thereby denies the authority of the state; if, on the other hand, he submits to the state and accepts its claim to authority, then so far as any of the above arguments indicate, he loses his autonomy.
>
> (*ibid.*, p. 40)

He similarly dismisses a defence of majoritarianism founded on a unanimous promise, in an original social contract, thenceforward to abide by merely majority decisions. 'If we hold that majority rule has some special validity, then it must be because of the character of majority rule itself, and not because of a promise which we may be thought to have made to abide by it' (*ibid.*, pp. 42–3). Wolff, however, is unable to find anything to meet this requirement, and though he feels there must be some solution to the original problem (*ibid.*, p. 78) he does not provide one. His championing of moral autonomy causes him to abandon democracy in favour of becoming what he calls a 'philosophical anarchist' (*ibid.*, p. viii).

Wolff sets out his claims by reference to the three abstract models of democratic decision-making which I have described. For the course of my own argument it is important to point out that in fact we have a total of four possible models under consideration, as set out in fig. 1. Decision-making can directly

	DIRECT	REPRESENTATIVE
UNANIMOUS	U D √ √	U R √ ×
MAJORITARIAN	M D × √	M R × ×

Fig.1 Features of Wolff's four models and their acceptability

involve the entire populace or it can be the prerogative of a sub-section of the populace, representatives; and decisions may require either unanimous or merely majority support. This gives us the four abstract models of unanimous direct democracy, unanimous representative democracy, majoritarian direct democracy and majoritarian representative democracy. In the diagram, a tick beneath a given feature indicates its acceptability according to Wolff's arguments and a cross its unacceptability. From this it will be seen that, on Wolff's original arguments, all the models except unanimous direct democracy stand condemned, but that the model to which existing liberal democracies most closely approximate, majoritarian representative democracy, has *most* to be said against it.

2

Wolff's critics have clearly thought that the position I have outlined admits of fairly easy refutation on a number of connected grounds. In the present section I merely set out their arguments, with a minimum of critical comment, in order to exhibit their interconnection.

First, there is the question of the supposed *scope* of state authority. It has been objected that no serious theorist would argue that we have an obligation to obey the state *whatever it may command*. Even Hobbes, after all, thought there were limits in this respect (Bates 1972, p. 177). It is reasonable to suppose that most defenders of state authority would place far stricter limits on its scope than Hobbes, and at the very least there are certain areas, for example freedom of thought and discussion, where a strong argument can be advanced for the immorality of being prepared to accept the state's authority whatever it might conceivably command (Dworkin 1971, pp. 566–7). To the extent, therefore, that Wolff argues against this unreasonably extreme view of the scope of state authority it has been objected that he fails to engage with real opponents at all.

Perhaps of more central importance (but also connected with this) is the question of the *grounds* of state authority. Again, it has seemed to Wolff's critics unrealistic of him to imagine an opponent who thinks he has a duty to obey the law *merely because it is the law* (e.g. Smith 1973, pp. 294–5). It would be more accurate to say that the opponent would recognise a *prima facie* obligation to obey the law (Bates 1972, p. 178), or that he would regard the legitimacy of the laws of the state as 'simply one morally relevant factor figuring in his determination of his moral obligation' (Reiman 1972, p. 38).

Even this, however, can come to seem a misleading way of expressing the matter, for it may be thought to suggest, falsely, that the mere property of being the law carries all on its own some magical force for the process of moral assessment, decision and action. But this is not so, and no one thinks it to be so, it has been objected. Rather, any moral legitimacy which a state's law has it has because ordinary, general moral considerations apply to it. And the complaint has been made, for example by Reiman

(1978, pp. 107–8), that it is precisely a justification of the law by reference to such general considerations which Wolff had stigmatised as irrelevant to his problem (Wolff 1970, p. 40). He has therefore tied his opponent's hands and gained only a hollow victory by declaring that 'appeal to the moral benefits of a political system are ruled out of court' (Reiman 1978, p. 108). Small wonder, then, that Wolff cannot find a justification for state power when he has disqualified from consideration the only area where such a justification can be found.

Once it is recognised that such an appeal is *in* order then, so it is suggested, we can see that those very same considerations which serve to make a system of laws legitimate, namely its moral effects, will also serve as reasons (though not conclusive ones) for obeying those laws (Reiman 1972, p. 54; Reiman 1978, pp. 106–7).

At this point a number of critics have claimed to detect a further weakness in Wolff's position. They have argued that although there is obviously an overlap between the question of the state's legitimate authority and an individual's obligation to obey the law, there is not perfect coincidence (Reiman 1972, p. 44; cf. Pritchard 1973, p. 298). I can recognise that the moral benefits of having a system of laws are sufficiently great as to legitimate state authority, and I can recognise on the same grounds that there is something to be said in general for conforming to such laws; but in a particular case I can still make my own decision whether to conform. As an individual, having taken into account in my deliberations the legitimate claims of the law, I can still decide for myself what is right and how I ought to behave. In this process, therefore, my autonomy is not infringed, and Wolff's original confrontation between state authority and individual autonomy proves to have been too stark (Pritchard 1973, p. 299; Bates 1972, p. 178; Frankfurt 1973, p. 411).

Finally, it has been pointed out that there was in any case an ambiguity in Wolff's original project (Martin 1974, p. 141). Sometimes it seemed that his aim was to show the *practical* impossibility of reconciling authority and autonomy, even though the model of unanimous direct democracy was allowed as a theoretical resolution (Wolff 1970, p. 27). Sometimes it seemed that he wished to show the *conceptual* impossibility of any resolution, as when he says that the state where authority and autonomy are reconciled 'must be consigned to the category of the round square' (*ibid.*, p. 71).

Now I noted earlier that Wolff himself subsequently retracted the claim that the model of unanimous direct democracy provided a resolution. But his word is not the last word: his critics have preferred to think that it does provide a resolution, and one which can be extended. If my autonomy is unimpaired and I do become bound by a decision taken in accordance with a principle I agreed to earlier, why should the same not be true of *other* circumstances where I begin by giving my allegiance to some principle, such as the principle of majority voting (Dworkin 1971, p. 564)? After all, Wolff himself even recognises cases where my autonomy is unimpaired by my taking orders from someone, for example a doctor or a ship's captain during a shipwreck (Wolff 1970, pp. 15–16). If that is correct, why should it not be possible to mobilise a similar argument in the infinitely more important case of obeying the state (Frankfurt 1973, pp. 409–11)?

Alternatively, it has been objected that Wolff has not done enough to sustain a claim that any resolution is conceptually impossible. For this, he would have to do more than point to existing states and show that they involve the domination of some people by others: he would have to show that there *cannot be* a state where individuals act as public agents expressing the common will of the whole people rather than in a private capacity (Reiman 1978, pp. 103–4).

Some of these points may very well constitute valid objections to Wolff's position if it is taken *au pied de la lettre*. I now attempt to pursue the argument further by showing that they are less than compelling on a more charitable interpretation of his argument.

3

First, is it fair to say that Wolff ties his opponent's hands by arbitrarily excluding any defence of the state based on its moral benefits? In fact, he had argued that a defence based on *good effects* was unsatisfactory, on the grounds that this would leave the democratic state with no special status. If we claim, for example, that the state's authority is legitimate because it advances the general welfare, we face the possibility that this might be truer of a benevolent dictatorship than a democratic state (cf. Wolff 1970, p. 40). To this may be added Wolff's further point that a defence based on good effects leaves no point to classical democratic theory, with its insistence on the importance of a social contract. That is, if the state's authority can be justified by reference to its consequences, why bother to construct arguments which seek to show that in some way the governed have *consented* to be governed (cf. Wolff 1976, p. 87)?

Now admittedly Wolff's points here are themselves less than compelling. So much the worse for classical democratic theory, someone might say, if it attempted a defence based on shadowy promises when it did not need to do so. And democracy will be left with no special status only if it is *true* that the general welfare would be advanced more under a benevolent dictatorship – which is at best a speculative and dubious proposition. All the same, I believe there is more to be said on Wolff's side, of a kind which allows better sense to be made of his saddling his opponent with the view that one should obey the law because it is the law.

It may be that there are some defenders of democracy who are prepared to rest their defence on contingent claims about the consequences which follow from that form of social organisation. But there are surely others who would be reluctant to leave it *open to question* whether it was morally preferable to a dictatorship. They would wish to argue that *in itself* democracy is to be preferred, perhaps on grounds to do with its giving appropriate dignity or an equal say to all people in deciding the social arrangements under which they are to live (cf. Graham 1976, pp. 231–2). But this is precisely what Wolff explicitly denies. He argues that when all questions of long-term consequences, side-effects, etc. of obeying the laws of a state have been settled, there is no force at all in going on to say: 'And furthermore this is a legitimate state, because it is a democracy' (Wolff 1973, pp. 303–4). My suggestion is that in taking up this position Wolff is engaging with a real and genuinely held opposing view. His opponent can now be seen not as someone mindlessly obsessed with obeying the law merely because it is the law, but mindfully concerned with obeying a law because it is the law of a democratic state. If the democratic state is based on majority rule, it is perfectly fair and sensible to challenge such a man, as Wolff does, to say what it is about majority rule itself which gives it any special validity (Wolff 1970, pp. 42–3). If an answer is elaborated along the lines I suggested (in terms of dignity and an equal say in social arrangements) Wolff's further challenge concerning the forfeiture of autonomy will also have to be met. But at this stage neither side can plausibly claim that its view is just obviously correct. The nature of 'the democratic state' would have to be far more completely specified, as would Wolff's notion of autonomy and his reasons for assigning supreme importance to it. But the interim verdict, at least, must be that Wolff has not unfairly ruled out of court the arguments of his opponent; rather, he has pointed out that an appeal to extraneous consequences will not do all the work required of a certain kind of defender of democracy.

At this point it might be replied that this defence will still bring us no nearer to establishing Wolff's central claim. If, as was argued earlier, he conflates the question of the state's legitimacy with the question whether an individual can accept democratic decision-making, then the points he makes about justifying the state's authority will not show that acceptance of democratic decisions involves forfeiture of autonomy, especially if we bear in mind that no real opponent will think that *anything* which the state might command should be accepted.

But again there is more to be said on the Wolffian side. If 'acceding to what the majority decides *within certain limits* need not involve a surrender of autonomy' (Bates 1972, p. 179), what are those limits to be? There is one answer to this which is clearly inadequate and leads straight back to Wolff's problem. This is to suggest that the individual's right to decide for himself whether he should obey the state's command is exhausted in satisfying himself that the command does meet 'various procedural requirements and conform with various principles of limit and exclusion' (Frankfurt 1973, p. 411). For if *that* is all the discretion I have, then, as Frankfurt immediately goes on to say:

'The citizen does agree, of course, to comply with decisions that he himself may think wrong or unwise' (*ibid.*). Perhaps it is true that this 'hardly amounts to the wholesale abandonment of human dignity' (*ibid.*), but if it merits the description of acquiescing in something you believe to be wrong, then there is still a case to answer.

On this interpretation Wolff's argument would connect with Wollheim's 'paradox of democracy' as noted by Bates (1972, p. 178). If I believe that whatever is democratically decided ought to be enacted, and if I also hold particular views about what ought to be enacted, then there is the permanent possibility of a conflict. As an individual I may believe that A ought to be enacted and as a democrat I may have committed myself to the view that B (which was democratically decided) ought to be enacted. I have argued elsewhere that, though this is not a paradox, it is a problem (Graham 1976). Wolff's challenge lies in his view that the conditions of taking moral autonomy seriously preclude the problem from arising in the first place. Whereas in Wollheim's original account we are presumed to feel the pull of the commitment both to (*a*) our own particular views on questions of social policy and to (*b*) what the majority opts for, Wolff thinks that the conditions of being a serious moral agent dictate that our commitment to our own moral views should fill all the available space. For him there is no paradox because the dilemma turns out to have only one horn.

There is at least a *prima facie* plausibility in Wolff's insistence that we should above all decide for ourselves when something is morally wrong, and have no part of it. It seems to me unlikely that the further conclusions he draws, concerning obligation to the state, can be successfully resisted merely by making stipulations about the limits of such an obligation. Maintaining that it exists only when what the state commands has conformed to procedural requirements, etc. leaves us with Wolff's problem; maintaining that it exists only where the individual sees nothing wrong with what is required of him or her would indeed obviate Wolff's problem, but only at the cost of throwing doubt on whether such an attitude betokens serious acceptance of any form of democratic decision-making. Imagine, for example, a colleague who says he will accept the democratic decisions of the faculty, as determined by majority vote, as long as he does not think those decisions are morally wrong. This is, to be sure, not *quite* the same as committing oneself to abide by decisions only when they coincide with one's own view – for there might be a majority decision in favour of some course of action about which one was morally indifferent. But that is not the hard case for testing whether someone is really a democrat. The hard case is one where I do have strong feelings which differ from those of the majority. If, as a general policy, I always give priority to my strong feelings on such occasions, my commitment to democracy is dubious in the extreme. There may be a resolution of this problem, but it is a genuine one.

Incidentally, on this construction of Wolff's argument it is possible to make better sense of his describing his opponent as having a commitment to obey the state *whatever may be commanded*. So far we have taken this to signify an *unlimited* obligation, a position we agreed to be unrealistic and not likely to be held by anyone. But an alternative is to construe the phrase as signifying not so much that this is an unlimited obligation as that 'whatever may be commanded' is a variable many of whose values I do not know in advance. And there is certainly plausibility in saying that an individual who takes seriously his role as an autonomous moral agent cannot give so many hostages to fortune. For he will indeed then be subscribing to what Reiman calls a 'wild card morality', that is 'a morality in which a moral obligation to do something exists, while the nature of that "something" can be filled in later' (Reiman 1972, p. 2). Reiman may think that such a morality is absurd, but in that case it looks as though subscription to abiding by democratic decisions is absurd – a result which ought to displease Reiman as much as it would please Wolff.

As to the question whether Wolff's thesis is properly construed as casting doubt on the practical or the logical impossibility of reconciling individual autonomy and state authority, at this stage in the argument it is not possible to give a decisive answer. Much turns on what we make of the arguments concerning the model of unanimous direct democracy and the cases where Wolff allows that it may be rational to forfeit autonomy (see section 4). Much also turns on what we make of comments, such as Frankfurt's, that this form as described by Wolff (1970, pp. 24–5) 'is very much like what we have, or are in principle supposed to have, now' (Frankfurt 1973, p. 414). Unless the parenthesis is given sufficient weight as completely to cancel out what precedes it, this remark strikes me as extraordinary in its failure to appreciate the chasm between Wolff's model and contemporary American or British society. If unanimous direct democracy is the only available solution there is at least a huge and apparently insurmountable practical problem. And if Reiman is correct in holding that for the state to be something other than the organised domination of some by others it must be possible for individuals to act according to rules expressing the *common will of the whole people* (Reiman 1978, pp. 103–4), then indeed unanimous direct democracy does look like the only solution. In short, Wolff's argument throws down a challenge to defenders of the authority of actual states to justify the rhetoric in which their defence is often couched ('the will of the people', etc.) and perhaps to show good cause why we should not insist that such rhetoric be taken literally.

One further point on the relevance of Wolff's argument to practical possibilities. Reiman is careful to dissociate himself from any argument about the legitimacy of existing states (*ibid.*, p. 101 n. 15), but he argues: 'Regardless of what presidents or dictators may claim, no state needs to claim a moral right to its subjects' mindless obedience to qualify as legitimate . . .' (*ibid.*, p. 99). This may be true, but it is the demand for obedience (whether mindless or not) against one's better judgement which is in question, and it is not merely presidents and dictators who demand and enforce this. It takes perhaps only a little more imagination than that displayed by Wolff's critics to realise that one would receive very short shrift in a court of law if one attempted to explain that on this occasion one had come to the conclusion that, all things considered, it was not wrong to break the law and that in the circumstances the state had no right to take any untoward action against one. Indeed, this is not a matter of speculation but of recorded historical fact, in such cases as the appeal involved in *Chandler et al.* v. *DPP* (*1964 Appeal Cases*, pp. 763ff). The appellants were nuclear disarmers who announced in advance their intention to enter an RAF airfield and immobilise it by sitting on it. They were charged with conspiring to commit a breach of Section 1 of the Official Secrets Act 1911, namely for a purpose prejudicial to the safety or interests of the state to enter a Royal Air Force station. In the course of their trial the judge refused to allow counsel for the defence to cross-examine or call evidence as to the appellants' beliefs that their acts would benefit the state or to show that the appellants' purpose was not in fact prejudicial to the safety or interests of the state. An appeal was lodged partly on the grounds that the judge was wrong to exclude such evidence. It was dismissed by the Court of Criminal Appeal, where it was stated that '. . . the appellants and any experts called for them are not qualified to give expert opinion on the general policy of this country' (*ibid.*, p. 770). The House of Lords concurred. (In the memorable words of Lord Reid, '. . . the interests of the majority are not necessarily the same as the interests of the state' *ibid.*, p. 790).

The state, in the form of its most important legal institutions, does demand obedience, and rules as irrelevant the grounds someone might have for exercising individual discretion. So far as existing forms of state are concerned, it is arguable that practically speaking this could not be otherwise. Wolff himself has often been criticised for a lack of realism, but on the issue of what is permitted by way of individual discretion it seems to me that it is his critics who are at fault.

To conclude this part of my discussion, I have tried to show that Wolff's argument is not the easy target which it has often been taken to be. Two further stages are necessary in my own discussion before we can finally decide whether it is sound. First, we must consider whether its sting can be drawn on the basis of the concessions which Wolff himself makes in the course of his argument. Secondly, we have to broach broader issues and decide whether Wolff's own concessions are all they should be, given his own starting-point.

4

In his original text Wolff discusses three instances where it may not be appropriate for me to decide for myself in a particular situation what is the best thing to do. There is the model of unanimous direct democracy, as in the example where we all vote for economic conflicts to be settled according to some principle and a particular application of the principle happens to disadvantage me (Wolff 1970, pp. 22–7). There is the case where I take orders from a competent doctor in a course of treatment (*ibid.*, p. 15). And there is the case where I take orders from a ship's captain in an emergency because everyone else is doing so (*ibid.*, pp. 15–16). Critics have thought that the concessions made here may be utilised in showing the legitimacy of state authority (e.g. Dworkin 1971, pp. 563–4; Frankfurt 1973, pp. 409–11). I suggest that it is proper to make such concessions, but the further desired conclusion does not follow.

Wolff himself actually wavers over the question of forfeiting autonomy. On the one hand he says: 'From the example of the doctor, it is *obvious* that there are at least some situations in which it is reasonable to give up one's autonomy' (Wolff 1970, p. 15; my emphasis). On the other, he later remarks: 'It is perfectly possible to forfeit autonomy, as we have already seen. Whether it is wise, or good, or right to do so is, of course, *open to question* . . .' (*ibid.*, p. 41; my emphasis). However, it seems clear that in these cases there *are* grounds for relinquishing individual discretion. The precise circumstances of the unanimous direct democracy model are important. Along with everyone else I vote for a certain *principle* for settling conflicts. In a particular case its application *disadvantages* me, but I still think the principle fair. Here, it is reasonable to insist that I should accept whatever the arbitration body decides in applying those principles even though I do not *like* it. Both here and in the other cases I have a fairly precise and specific idea what it is I am commanded to do – and have no independent objections to doing it. (We may assume the doctor says 'Take these pills three times a day. They will kill the virus and have no harmful side-effects', rather than 'Jump into this vat of boiling oil. The pain will go immediately.')

It is these features which give grounds for obedience here;[2] but

[2] The case of unanimous direct democracy does not strictly involve a sacrifice of autonomy. Since I still think the arbitration principles fair I am simply bound by an arrangement *I myself* think correct. That is presumably one reason why

it is precisely these features which are not present in existing, large-scale political arrangements. In a representative democracy, for example, new issues come up and I neither know nor have had any say in the principles on which they will be decided. I have only had the opportunity to vote for an individual who will have such a say, and my vote will have been cast on the most general of platforms, which may in any case subsequently be abandoned. I therefore forfeit my autonomy over a very wide area, with no certain knowledge on what principles decisions will be taken by an individual who is not likely to be well known personally to me (cf. Scanlon 1972, p. 166). In all these respects the situation is very different from those limited examples with which we began. Here I am expected to sign a blank cheque and, as we have seen earlier, it is against just such a practice that the substance of Wolff's argument is directed.

The special and limited nature of the cases discussed, then, suggests that there is no easy transition from them to an argument for a wholesale abandonment of autonomy. There may be such an argument: a man might, for example, come to believe that all his particular moral decisions were disasters and for that reason look around for some other procedure for reaching them. He might then follow Dworkin's suggestion that there are 'wise men, novelists and saints' (Dworkin 1971, p. 565) from whom he can learn. But unless he trusts his own judgement in deciding which of his fellow human beings fit this description he is going to have to take their word for it. Personally, I should doubt whether anyone who *claimed* the title of wise man or saint was entitled to it. And there remains the problem whether the professional politicians who in fact make decisions on the citizens' behalf fall into either of these categories as a general rule. In the absence of some reliable signs indicating who is fitted for the role of philosopher king, there remains considerable appeal in Wolff's argument that we are no better than children if we willingly allow others to determine how we

Wolff no longer regards the case as a solution to the conflict between autonomy and authority. It would be interesting to know his view of the distinct case where I genuinely *change my mind* about what is a fair set of principles. Can I now be bound by a view which I adhered to at an earlier moment? There are difficult problems here, for Wolff and everyone else, about obligation over time: see Perkins 1972.

shall behave (Wolff 1970, p. 72). That position seems to me to be more dignified and less frightening than the view that a responsible person may prefer not to have an opinion on the question of nuclear weapons policy because there are other important things in life (Frankfurt 1973, p. 408).

5

Where do we turn at this point, if we do not wish simply to accept Wolff's conclusion that the conditions for being a responsible moral agent preclude acceptance of any form of democratic decision-making? One thing we might do is cast around for a model of democratic decision-making which is distinct from the four outlined in section 1 and which escapes his criticisms. Alternatively, we might challenge more directly the central role which Wolff allots to the principle of autonomy, or at least press for many more details of the entire ethical theory which he admitted he had taken for granted.

Neither of these strategies as such looks particularly attractive. It may appear that the four models already described actually exhaust the field: for surely, in a democracy, either we (the populace) or someone representing us must make the decisions, and surely those decisions must be accepted either by all or by most people? Even if there is some fifth model to be described (as I shall later argue there is), there is no guarantee that it will avoid the main thrust of Wolff's argument. On the other hand, if we are to disentangle truth from falsity in the longstanding problem of moral autonomy we shall at the very least have an extremely large task to perform. Accordingly, I opt for a more limited strategy. I believe that in the end *some* principle of autonomy similar to that propounded by Wolff is acceptable; I have found many difficulties in arriving at a satisfactory formulation of the principle, however; and I shall not attempt to do so now. Instead, I want to draw out some of the implications of Wolff's version of the principle and to suggest that, when they are understood, the principle can be seen not merely not to preclude acceptance of majoritarianism, but actually to require such acceptance. It should by now be clear that Wolff holds the principle in a particularly strong form. If *his* version allows acceptance of majoritarianism, then *a fortiori* some weaker and more satisfactory version of the principle should do so.

We know from the discussion so far that Wolff thinks we *can* abandon our autonomy and (though he wavers on this) that there is sometimes good reason to do so. Although in general a rational agent should make his or her own decision about what is right, there are some particular circumstances where it is sensible not to do so. *Sometimes it is rational to forfeit autonomy.* That is the point which matters for the moment. It is reached, amongst other things, via a consideration of situations where someone has expertise which I lack, and this almost invites a critic to utilise it in the service of a bad argument resting on the assumption that there are (in the relevant sense) political experts. But the way in which the point is reached does not concern me. That it is reached at all makes it clear, as I suggested in section 1, that Wolff thinks autonomy is to be *maximised.* Forfeiture of autonomy is to be kept to a minimum, rather than avoided altogether. This is important because it distinguishes Wolff's position from a side-constraint view of autonomy, at least if side-constraints are taken to be absolute (cf. Nozick 1974, pp. 28–30). A course of action, or the pursuit of some goal, is not automatically ruled out because it involves some forfeiture of autonomy.

It is at this point that I wish to avoid the long argument over whether democracy provides a context where a goal may be pursued at the expense of autonomy, in favour of arguing that the form in which Wolff holds the principle of autonomy *itself* provides an argument to that end. The two features of the principle which I think license this claim are its *universality* and its connection with *action*.

Wolff thinks that it is supremely important for the moral agent to maximise autonomous decisions. It would, of course, be missing his point hugely to ask: '*Which* moral agent?' My autonomy is important not because it is mine, but because it is that of a being possessed of free will and reason (cf. Wolff 1970, p. 13). Wolff takes it as one of his fundamental assumptions that men in general fall under this description (*ibid.*, p. 12). The only categories of human being he explicitly excludes are 'children and madmen' (*ibid.*); and though the ageism is deliberate I take it the sexism is not, and that we can conclude that Wolff wishes to allow all sane, adult members of the human race to come within the scope of his remarks. What is important to Wolff, therefore, is that the autonomy of *all* moral agents should be maximised. Consistency requires, and I take it that as a good Kantian Wolff would not wish to deny, that he must universalise his position. It is important that he, *qua* responsible moral agent, should take his own moral decisions, and it is *equally* important that anyone relevantly similar should also do so.

In order to see the importance of action in the statement of the principle of autonomy, consider the following situation. We live in a society ruled over by a dictator. He tells us that he has been entirely convinced by Wolff's argument: in consequence, he will allow each of us to decide for ourselves in any particular situation what we ought to do. Of course, he adds, since he is the dictator he has no intention of allowing us to *do* what we decide we ought to do, and he will ensure by coercion and the threat of coercion that we end up doing what *he* thinks we ought to do. Alternatively, consider an individual who claims to have been convinced by Wolff's argument. He no longer accepts that the state has any *de jure* authority over him and insists that he must reserve for himself the right to decide what he ought to do in particular circumstances. Invariably, he tells us, having exercised his autonomy in this way by making his own decision, he then does whatever his brother-in-law tells him to do. (His brother-in-law has a degree from Harvard.)

It is arguable that the descriptions of what is going on offered by the dictator and the individual are not even coherent. For example, it might be said that though the individual may *claim* that he arrives at his own decisions about what he ought to do, in fact his behaviour shows that what he really thinks is that he ought to do what his brother-in-law tells him. Whether that is correct or not, it seems fairly plain that we do not have here examples where Wolff's principle is being properly adhered to, and that the reason why this is so is that the protagonists stop short of allowing autonomous decisions to issue in action. As Wolff puts it, again echoing Kant, 'the responsible man arrives at moral decisions which he expresses to himself in the form of imperatives' (Wolff 1970, pp. 13–14). But since he is in the position both of issuing the imperatives and of being required to comply with them, he does not achieve autonomy merely in doing the first thing without the second: '. . . moral autonomy . . . is a *submission* to laws which one has made for oneself' (*ibid.*, p. 14; my emphasis).

Putting together the point about universality and the point about action we might express Wolff's concern with autonomy in this way: the decisions of rational moral agents are to be realised in action as often as possible, and it is immaterial *whose* autonomous moral decision is in question. Given the general grounds on which importance is attached to them in the first place, one has as much right as any other to a claim on our attention.

Now, once the form of the autonomy principle has been made explicit in these ways, we see a further reason for speaking only of the *maximisation* of autonomy. As social creatures we are necessarily involved in interaction with one another. Many of our important goals and projects will be joint ones requiring joint action. Even those which are strictly individual are likely to impinge on others, and theirs on us. This automatically brings with it the threat of a kind of conflict which brooks no evasion and also the threat that someone's autonomy will be thwarted. For whereas conflicting decisions can co-exist, conflicting actions which are the expression of such decisions cannot. I can decide that state of affairs S ought to obtain and you can decide that state of affairs not-S ought to obtain; but S and not-S cannot both be realised. Hence the autonomous decision of one of us will fail to get translated into action.

This gives an advocate of autonomy a strong motive for stressing the importance of discussion and debate, of canvassing and considering other views before making any final decision about what ought to happen and of exploring the possibilities for compromise. But such attempts to avoid conflict of the type specified may not always be successful. The question is, what do we do when they are not?

Or rather, what policy is dictated for someone who regards the principle of autonomy as supremely important? Suppose that everyone for whom it is appropriate to express a view on what state of affairs should obtain in a particular context has done so. (I leave aside the problem how we determine appropriateness.) Suppose, further, that all attempts at accommodation and compromise have been made in good faith and that that process is now at an end. And suppose that this has not issued in one universally held decision. Then we know that someone's autonomy will be thwarted. But, if my earlier argument was correct, it would be improper at this point to enter into a discussion about *whose* autonomy it should be: all are on equal terms as free, rational agents. What is required is maximisation of autonomy, indifferently to such questions of individuality. And that (I hope) suggests a rather obvious solution. The more decisions there are in favour of a given state of affairs obtaining, the more autonomy will be thwarted if that state of affairs is not brought about. Rational commitment to the autonomy principle, therefore, suggests that a state of affairs should not be brought about if there are fewer, rather than more, decisions to the effect that it should. Conversely, if most decisions *favour* a particular state of affairs, less damage will be caused to the maximisation of autonomy if that state of affairs is brought about rather than not. Or, to put it more simply, if you want to maximise autonomy where people disagree, accept majority votes.[3]

6

The picture of what is acceptable on Wolff's assumptions has changed from that described in section 1. It can now be presented as in fig. 2.

There are now *two* abstract models of social decision-making, acceptance of which is compatible with preserving autonomy to

[3] The most obvious way to attack my argument is by objecting that it takes no account of the *content* of the decisions in question, and that some of them, if given expression in action, might lead to the severe curtailment of other people's autonomy. This, of course, is one of the difficulties which crop up in the attempt to state the principle of autonomy in an acceptable form. Let me simply say here that it seems to me that this escape is unavailable to Wolff. To begin to discriminate amongst decisions in this way is implicitly to cease treating their authors as equal moral agents, and to come dangerously close to the position of the dictator of my earlier example.

	DIRECT	REPRESENTATIVE
UNANIMOUS	U D √ √	U R √ ×
MAJORITARIAN	M D √ √	M R √ ×

Fig. 2 Revised version of the acceptability of Wolff's four models

the greatest possible extent, namely unanimous direct democracy and also majoritarian direct democracy. Wolff himself eventually came to the view that though people may be bound by their collective commitments in unanimous direct democracy, this is still not creative of the political *authority* originally sought for (Wolff 1976, p. 88). This may be correct, and the same may be true of majoritarian direct democracy, but it is still true that these are procedures which a Wolffian ought to find acceptable. If so, we have moved a step further away from Wolff's own conclusion that the champion of autonomy must also be an anarchist.

But not far enough, it may be said. None of my arguments has shown the acceptability of *representation* in decision-making (and I have no others to offer).[4] So the model which approximates most closely to political reality still stands condemned, and all that has been salvaged is a model which is as unrealistic as Wolff's own original solution. In a large, complex world, what is the sense in talking of direct democracy as though we were all living in a tiny Athenian city-state?

There are two points to make in reply. In his 'Appendix: a proposal for instant direct democracy' (Wolff 1970, pp. 34–7) Wolff argues that the obstacles to the direct participation of all citizens in law-making are only technical, and he proposes a solution utilising modern technology which 'is meant a good deal more than half in earnest' (*ibid.*, p. 34). News programmes on television are to be replaced by briefing sessions, debates and

[4] For further comments on representative democracy, see Graham 1976, sections III and IV.

questions on matters for social decision, then once a week the whole populace votes on the current issues. This is a fantasy, of course. But it is instructive to consider *why* it is a fantasy, how far those aspects of life in modern society which make it a fantasy are irremovable, what concomitant social changes would have to take place to make Wolff's proposal more realistic and so on. Certainly Wolff's way of framing his point makes it clear that the question of what technology is available is highly pertinent for the issues here.[5]

But secondly, and more importantly, the options are not exhausted in the four models laid out in figs. 1 and 2. Hybrid and intermediate models are available which themselves approximate more or less closely to majoritarian direct democracy, and make it clear that abandonment of the idea that every appropriate person has a direct say on every issue does not imply acceptance of the representation we are familiar with. There are models, for example, where delegates take decisions on more or less clearly laid-down principles, where those decisions are open to more or less frequent scrutiny and ratification by the entire populace, and where the delegates themselves are subject to dismissal or more or less severe sanction depending on the degree of their departure from the principles in question. Such possible models are no doubt a long way from anything Wolff himself would find acceptable, but they are also a long way from existing representative systems, and their features and merits would repay investigation.

One final comment which connects with this. Wolff has been criticised for expressing his original views and subsequently defending them, on the grounds of the possible harm which this may produce. That is surely a mistake. Wolff belongs to a discipline which has a long and venerable tradition of following the argument wherever it leads, and if the unexamined life is not worth living it must be equally true that unthinking allegiance to the state is not worth giving. It is the merit of Wolff's arguments to cause us to look anew at the conventional wisdom of political passivity. When it is said that political systems begin from the

[5] For another interesting if frankly propagandist exploration, see Valinas 1978, and for some reservations, see Macpherson 1977.

assumption 'that some areas of behaviour are too crucial to the mutual well-being and survival of the community to be left to the consciences of its members' (Reiman 1972, p. 29) Wolff does well to point out that it is mystification to posit 'the state' as a solution to this problem (Wolff 1976, p. 97). For the alternative to leaving matters to the conscience of the members of society is leaving them to *some* of its members. And we must then face honestly the question *which* members are fitted for this role.

But if we are impressed by the challenge Wolff has laid down and unimpressed by ancient prejudices about the wickedness of human nature, there is no reason why the outcome of considering his arguments should be throwing bombs in the streets, or even a refusal to pay taxes. What remains is to consider further the different possible *forms* of democracy and decide whether they are all equally subject to Wolff's attack. Wolff thinks so, but he may be wrong, and he has at least broadened the possibilities which may be considered as attempts to improve on the problems presented by existing representative systems. Those systems may be infinitely preferable to the alternatives on offer in the world as we know it, but it would be hard to deny that they give the ordinary individual a relatively small degree of control over his or her conditions of existence. Anyone wishing to change that state of affairs for the better will have to be prepared to *argue* the matter. And they will need the help of all the rational autonomous agents they can lay their hands on.[6]

REFERENCES

Bates, S. 1972. Authority and autonomy. *Journal of Philosophy*, 69, pp. 175–9.

Dworkin, G. 1971. Review of R. P. Wolff: *In defense of anarchism*. *Journal of Philosophy*, 68, pp. 561–7.

Frankfurt, H. G. 1973. The anarchism of Robert Paul Wolff. *Political Theory*, 1, pp. 405–14.

Graham, K. 1976. Democracy, paradox and the real world. *Proceedings of the Aristotelian Society*, LXXXVI, pp. 227–45.

Macpherson, C. B. 1977. *The life and times of liberal democracy*. New York, Oxford University Press.

6 For helpful comments I am grateful to Alison Assiter, G. A. Cohen, Geoff Cupit, Alan Haworth, Trevor Pateman, Tony Skillen and David Watson.

Martin, R. 1974. Wolff's defence of philosophical anarchism. *Philosophical Quarterly*, 24, pp. 140–9.

Nozick, R. 1974. *Anarchy, state and Utopia*. Oxford, Blackwell.

Perkins, L. 1972. On reconciling autonomy and authority. *Ethics*, 82, pp. 114–23.

Pritchard, M. S. 1973. Wolff's anarchism. *Journal of Value Inquiry*, 7, pp. 296–302.

Reiman, J. H. 1972. *In defense of political philosophy*. New York, Harper and Row.

1978. Anarchism and nominalism: Wolff's latest obituary for political philosophy. *Ethics*, 89, pp. 95–110.

Scanlon, T. 1972. A theory of freedom of expression. *Philosophy and Public Affairs*, 1. In *The philosophy of law*, ed. R. Dworkin, pp. 153–71, Oxford University Press.

Smith, M. B. E. 1973. Wolff's argument for anarchism. *Journal of Value Inquiry*, 7, pp. 292–5.

Valinas, B. 1978. Democracy and the silicon chip. *Socialist Standard* (The Socialist Party of Great Britain), 74, pp. 170–1.

Wolff, R. P. 1970. *In defense of anarchism*. New York, Harper and Row.

1973. Reply to Pritchard and Smith. *Journal of Value Inquiry*, 7, pp. 303–6.

1976. A reply to Reiman. In *In defense of anarchism*, 2nd edn, pp. 83–113.

6 *Freedom of speech*

ANTHONY SKILLEN

> Whoever, in a public spot,
> Attempts to argue shall be shot
> To reason by gesticulation
> Will bring the self-same castigation
>
> Your mayor you must trust in blindly
> He guards the town and watches kindly
> With anxious care o'er old and young.
> Your duty is to hold your tongue.
>
> Heinrich Heine[1]

> The essence of censorship is based on the haughty conceit of a police state concerning its officials. The public is not given credit for having a sound mind and a good will to do the most simple thing. But even the impossible is to be possible for the officials.
>
> Karl Marx[2]

1

Many socialists regard freedom of speech as a value specific to bourgeois market liberalism and its Millian view of 'the free market in ideas'. It is also common for socialists to think that they should call for and actively engage in the suppression of the expression of racist, fascist, sexist and right wing views: 'no platform for fascists'. In this article I shall defend a libertarian position on speech in what I take to be socialist terms. This will involve criticising authoritarian schools of socialism as well as bourgeois liberalism. It will entail an examination of what 'speech' relevantly is and of the constituents and conditions of its freedom or unfreedom. If bourgeois liberty can be seen to be

[1] From 'A recollection of Krähwinkel's days of terror', Heine 1975, p. 166.
[2] 'Comments on the latest Prussian censorship introduction' (1842), in Easton and Guddat 1967, p. 91.

narrow and restricted it is, in my view, no part of socialist liberation to replace it with something even more 'pinched and hidebound'.

Within the liberal and especially the juridical frame of reference,[3] censorship and criminalisation of certain expressions are what constitutes interference with freedom of speech. Some writers restrict their attention, moreover, to *state* interference, arguing that in so far as freedom of speech is a *political* right it is a right specifically against the state. These views represent the open society's enemies far too narrowly, ignoring less formal economic and cultural dimensions of political freedom. It seems to me obvious that a society in which governments are permissive, but in which chanting, bullying, assaulting and book-burning (smoke-bombs were favoured by right wing authoritarians in my undergraduate days) are rampant is not one marked by freedom of speech. With this broad conception of what is at issue, I shall defend freedom of speech against what, in my experience, are common ways of arguing against it.

There is an *a priori* argument which even some 'I am-in-favour-of-free-speech-but' liberals express, directed at authoritarians of left or right. According to this, those who urge intolerance or unfreedom – such as fascists – thereby lose the right themselves to be tolerated. Karl Popper, in *The open society and its enemies*, for example, says that governments should 'tolerate all who are tolerant' (Popper 1962, p. 266). But is it right, as some argued against the South Place Ethical Society's allowing the National Front to use its premises, that 'those who would deny freedom to others have no right to freedom'?[4] It is true that the intolerant, or those who deny the value of tolerance or freedom, cannot themselves consistently appeal to 'freedom of speech' to defend their own propaganda against suppression. In this sense 'they cannot complain' against illiberal treatment. It does not follow, however, that upholders of freedom cannot object to illiberal treatment of the illiberal or that the illiberal have no political right of protest or appeal and ought not to be allowed to promote their illiberal views. They violate consisten-

[3] For example, Fried 1978, p. 82 and Scanlon 1977, pp. 153–71.
[4] See *The Guardian*, March 1980 for an extended discussion.

cy if they appeal in the name of freedom against suppression, but that is to transgress a logical, not a political rule. The illiberalism of a view no more justifies its suppression in the name of liberty than does the advocacy of torture merit torture in the name of humanity. Intolerance, injustice or cruelty do not justify, *a priori*, retributive intolerance, injustice or cruelty. The vision of a society in which only liberals have the right to liberty is conceptually as well as actually comic.[5]

But the fallacious argument sketched here derives persuasive force from more than confusions over self-refutation. It is often merged unnoticed with an empirical claim. Consider the slide from 'views opposed to freedom', in the sense of propositions denying that freedom is a good, to 'views opposed to freedom' in the sense of views the advocacy and acceptance of which harm free ways of life; a slide from propositional to causal relations. It is not uncommon for advocates of restriction to confuse these senses and to persuade themselves that it is self-evident that illiberal views harm liberty and therefore may be suppressed. Popper, for example, speaks of a 'paradox of tolerance': 'Unlimited tolerance *must* lead to the disappearance of tolerance', so that 'any movement preaching intolerance places itself outside the law' (Popper 1962, p. 265), while in the same passage stressing the contingent matter of *possible* illiberal consequences of freedom of speech for the illiberal – the movement could grow and crush free institutions. Clearly the causal and analytic issues are related – speech moves because of its content – but they are distinct: the advocacy of an illiberal position could strengthen freedom, through its manifest silliness, for example, or because its articulation forces its opponents to crystallise and deepen their position (compare Mill in *On liberty*). On the other hand, if actual menace to freedom were our criterion, libertarian views could in certain circumstances (warfare, for example) be argued to be in need of some restriction.

The above argument for censorship turned on the content or view expressed. But most serious argument turns on the issues of the role of speech in social life. According to the 'harm principle', harmfulness renders actions liable to restriction and,

[5] See Rawls 1972, p. 216 for a discussion of this issue.

according to some, speech which is or is likely to be harmful ought, like any other action, to be subject to restriction.[6] In the present context, the advocacy of racist, pro-fascist and sexist views could be said to be 'harmful'. It is to this difficult issue that I now turn.

It does not follow from an action's being harmful that it is right to suppress it. Suppression is, arguably, an evil in itself, simply *qua* restriction and frustration. Moreover, suppression is never a mere 'negation' of an act; it involves positive institutions and practices of formulating, judging and enforcing. As a general 'tactic', illiberalism in relation to speech can be dangerous to its advocates. 'No platform', 'smash the fascist' movements to suppress the expression of vicious viewpoints have helped bring about a general increase of law-and-order legislation aimed not so much at suppressing fascist groups as at imposing tighter state control of public space. The Public Order Act of 1936, present proposals to restrict public assembly, and the tendency for Chief Constables to ban all marches for extensive periods are examples. In that connection, it is not even surprising that the first conviction under the 1965 Race Relations Act was of a black man, found guilty of 'inciting race hatred' in such a way as to 'threaten a breach of the peace'.[7] Direct action to suppress opponents' expression, by mass picketing of halls, intimidation, physical attack or howling down provides a pretext, even a ground, for increased involvement in political life by the police. Calls for *state* legislation against vicious viewpoints, on the other hand, have to contend with the fact, not only that state law will be formulated in a *general* way, catching in its 'impartial' formulae friends as well as enemies, but that it establishes precedents to be followed up when the political climate changes: 'as we suppressed *that* menace to our constitution, so we must suppress *this* one'. In addition, the law must be formulated, interpreted and enforced by politicians, judges and police, with their own positions, traditions, prejudices and perspectives. Recognising the importance of considerations of this kind, John Locke made this question central to his *Letter concerning*

[6] See, for example, the Socialist Worker pamphlet *The fight against the racists; the National Front and how to smash it* (London) 1977.

[7] See, amongst others, MacDonald 1977, especially p. 139.

toleration: 'What power can be given to the magistrate for the suppression of an idolatrous church, which may not in time and place be made use of to the ruin of an orthodox one?' (Locke 1963, p. 67). Having scorned as 'liberalism' the defence of opponents' rights, having thus made some small contribution to the growth of illiberalism, one is then in a weak position to bewail the loss of 'democratic liberties' of movements one supports.

It is to the above kind of issue that Herbert Marcuse's argument for left 'intolerance' in 'Repressive tolerance' (Marcuse *et al.* 1965) is blind. Marcuse argued that modern capitalism is marked on the one hand by the orchestration of a standardised consensual ideology in line with the needs of the corporate state; on the other hand by bombardment of people with an array of 'points of view' which, like commodities, are presented as equally valid objects of 'choice'. The consequent conformism and irrationalism meant that the conditions of liberal democracy were absent:

> Where society has entered the phase of total administration and indoctrination this [the number of people 'qualified' to judge 'for the society as a whole' on matters of 'progress' and 'regress'] would be a small number indeed. The problem is not that of an educational dictatorship, but that of breaking the tyranny of public opinion and its makers in the closed society. (Marcuse 1965, p. 120)

Hence 'liberating tolerance would mean intolerance against movements from the right and toleration of movements from the left', 'stopping the words and images which feed this (mass) consciousness' (*ibid.*, pp. 122–3) and hence overturning oppression at the 'Archimedean point' (*ibid.*, p. 125) of consciousness. Marcuse exemplifies the kind of idealism criticised above in treating the act of suppression as if it stood outside the causal processes – of 'harm' – in which his target is located. Hence he fails to discuss what, assuming that society's masses are as doped and duped as he claims, would be the natural upshot of the 'left intolerance' he advocates. Given that 'public opinion' is so orchestrated, any act violating the interests of the controlling corporations can successfully be presented not, as Marcuse sees it, as valid by 'demonstrable criteria' (*ibid.*, p. 134) (demonstrable by whom to whom?), but as mad, vicious, dangerous, arbitrary, bestial or whatever epithet best suits the powers-that-be. In other words, given that things are as hopelessly bad as Marcuse claims, his remedy could have no other consequence than to make them worse. His errors are a reminder that in the battle for ideas, ideas about what the battlers are doing are not confined to the principal antagonists, but are structured with important consequences by the cultural environment in which the struggle takes place.

The above arguments could be said to be 'external' as well as 'negative' grounds against interference with speech. They address issues of harm likely to be done by restriction, and many of these harms are common to any restriction: not just on speech. They could be argued to be necessary costs and dangers that censorship entails. But freedom of speech can be a central value, something Voltaire was supposed to be ready to 'defend to the death', only if speech is a central human activity. This banality merits assertion because some libertarian arguments seem to depend precisely on the insignificance of speech: 'let them sound off'; 'it is only talk'; 'there is no evidence that such material influences conduct'. A libertarian position based on such views appears as one of 'indifferentism', in which tolerating is equated with ignoring. But if speech makes so little difference its freedom does not matter much either way, save that suppression will cause frustration and will, as we saw above, augment the power of the suppressing agency. It is not difficult, however, to see why this trivialising position tempts libertarianism. For if speech is central and often politically decisive, then speech which proclaims what is evil can be dangerous. From Plato to Marcuse, the potency of speech is given as the principal ground for its control. So, libertarians have to be aware that they are defending freedom of speech in the teeth of its dangerous power. What this requires, I think, is an account which stresses the centrality of the freedom for minds to be spoken, thoughts to be expressed, to the autonomy, dignity and rationality of members of a community, hence, with all its risks, as necessary to a community's being free, democratic and just. Throughout the ages, freedom of speech has been advocated as essential to the rational autonomy of belief and action: 'the liberty to know and argue' has been defended 'above all liberties' (Milton, *Areopagitica*) because speech is both the *expression* of thinking and the *vehicle* bringing minds into contact with each others' thinking, hence with 'ideas' on which to base thought and action.

To be silenced, to have one's views prevented from expression, is different from having them criticised, even severely. Similarly, to be kept from hearing opinions is different from being shown their errors. One's beliefs are close to the centre of 'who one is' and criticism of them can cut deep and meet protective resistance. But it is of the essence of human rationality that beliefs are held as valid, as justified by their correspondence to what is the case. The mind expresses itself and thus exposes itself to change through criticism. Criticism and discussion respect these dimensions of rationality, whereas silencing smashes at them, practically denying the capacity, not only to have reached views through some process of experience and reflection, but to go beyond them through further formative activity. This contempt applies also to your status as 'hearer' of speech, denying your capacity to reason and reflect on what you hear. You are treated as if words could causally affect you in an almost physical way rather than through their according with your grasp of things and thus their being 'acceptable' to you.

This 'cognitive' dimension of speech, or rather, the centrality of that dimension to speech, is part of what distinguishes it from other kinds of action. If I am prevented from 'doing something', I am not necessarily prevented thereby from openly arguing the case for being able to do that thing. I can even accept that some things to which I can see no objection are, having been deemed by a reasonable process in which I was able to participate to be objectionable, things which I cannot do. But if I am told that I cannot present or discuss my core beliefs because they are disgusting or vile or dangerous or simply false, then I am, to that extent, placed outside the community, able to move normally within it only through adopting a hypocritical mask: I am 'alienated' in a way that I cannot, it seems, rationally consent to.

This alienation, aside from its intrinsic evils, has consequences. When liberals 'wetly' describe censorship as 'counterproductive', they are expressing a causal truth rooted in the nature of speech as the mind's voice: that more or less rational creatures, prevented from uttering or hearing a view, will tend to infer, not that that view is wicked or deluded, but rather that it must have rational attractions which (rational) authoritarians are frightened to permit to be exposed to view. To say this is not to deny that a degree of thought-control is possible; but it is a reminder that ideas are not surgically killed off or intimidated out of existence by censorship – that a censored opinion does not respond to blockage as a suppressed 'physical' deed does. To adopt an appropriate Freudian expression, 'the repressed', in the form of more or less elaborated systems of ideas (good or bad), live on in an ignored and uncriticised underground and sub-cultural, 'ghetto', form, sometimes 'returning' to take the *status quo* by shocking surprise. Such is the 'cognitive' location of speech, then, that the suppression of expression tends both to reinforce the constricted beliefs and to place those whose speech is repressed in the position of 'aliens' in relation to the suppressors. This suggests that the strategy of strengthening the weapons of criticism may be superior for socialists to that of trying to eliminate their targets by force.

In urging this 'rationalist' position, I am contesting a view which treats, say, working-class youth as blindly 'vulnerable' to racist poison, a view which not only fails to do justice to the kinds of attraction racism has, but which sits uneasily with its characteristic classmate: the idea that racist thugs should be treated like dangerous animals, as if people can metamorphose from being sheep to being wolves. If animal metaphors are dangerous, in this area of stereotypy especially, so of course are medical metaphors. But, rather than simply denying that racism can be seen as a 'disease' or a 'poison', as if the acceptance of that vocabulary would *eo ipso* justify physico-chemical 'treatment' (amputation? isolation? inoculation? liquidation? purgation?), I would suggest that we might ask: what is the force of these metaphors in the realm of ideas? After all, amputation, immunisation and so on operate medically at the level appropriate to their target – penicillin kills bacteria. So we are left with the question: what *sort* of treatment (war, attack, etc.) is appropriate to this kind of disease (enemy, threat)? And we might then begin to see for example that 'preventive medicine' ceases to be a term incorporating a specific quasi-physical prescription, but one which opens up the whole question of the genesis and flourishing of ideas in society. We don't have to believe in Plato's *Republic* if we find the idea of spiritual and cultural *health* appealing. And we can learn from the limitations of medicine in its own domain too – some diseases are caused by cures.

Suppressed modes of expression then, 'which they won't let us come out in the open with', lead a rebellious under-life as hidden 'truths'. Generally speaking, legislation outlawing racist (compare blasphemous) speech, almost universally welcomed in liberal and left circles, is almost never invoked, serving little other function than to sophisticate rhetoric and to 'define' the society, for the appeasement of liberal consciences, as opposed to racism, thus fostering hypocrisy and illusion.[8] Meanwhile, racist immigration laws, police racism, which includes indifference to the physical safety of black people in Britain, and a press which treats blacks as non-existent save when they commit crimes, gave a less nominal definition of the establishment's priorities.

It was into such a self-deceived, hushed-up edifice that Enoch Powell marched, exposing under his own distorting light what had been swept under the carpet. More important than his so-called 'logic' or 'rhetorical power' in stirring the racist resentments of the English masses was the previous cloak of deceitful silence with which issues of race, immigration and social change in Britain had been covered. Powell's 'honesty' appeared certified by the shock-horror attempts at suppression, which aimed largely to lay the carpet back over the exposed conflicts. Similarly, the outrage which greeted the appearance inside school gates of socialist and fascist literature – 'politics!' – attested not to the concern for education but to the law and order pacification that goes by that name in our schools.[9]

[8] This 'expressionist' view of law is criticised in Skillen 1980. It is relevantly illustrated by Clor 1969, where it is claimed that legal expressions of 'what the community *is* committed to . . . must have an effect upon the moral attitudes of the people' (p. 194).

[9] This is illustrated by the difficulty of Professor Bernard Crick and others' attempt to get the serious study and discussion of politics, as distinct from 'civics', on to the school curriculum in England.

Censorship is indulged in as a desperate mark that 'we take this extremely seriously', and opponents of censorship are castigated for promoting indifference. But it is censorship which, by presenting an *image* of pre-established righteousness, saves teachers the task of grappling with political education, with developing critical capacities to see through vicious and obscurantist ideas through the difficult process of engaging in dialogue and being subject to refutation. To silence beliefs or dispositions-to-beliefs as beyond discussion or criticism is, as I have argued, to 'alienate'. A specific comment is in order here that, in general, racism is the ideology of the excluded, a way of seeing the world in which you are defined as belonging through the exclusion of others. Excluding the racist, then, exhibits a certain poetic justice, but is more deeply characterised as playing the same game – as making the world out to be a safer place for democracy than it is.

There is a tendency to treat speech as a mere vehicle conveying ideas from one mind to another. There is also a tendency, powerful in Marxist circles, to treat speech mainly as a means to provide information relevant to 'action'. But communities are not aggregates of 'theoretical' or 'practical' egos, any more than they are mobs of yes-men. Being able to hear, to get a hearing and reflect on ideas constitutes part of the good of membership in a community, part of what makes up people's social, yet individual, identities. The loss of 'identity' consequent on the suppression of the expression of one's views is not merely a frustration – it could be responded to with dull, 'painless', apathy, the 'mental torpor' that Mill derided in *On liberty*, or with withdrawal into an alienated sub-community. It is a violation of one's status as an active political animal, sharing in the life of the community by communicating and responding to views about its proper conduct.

In assuming that a plurality of opposed views and interests are part of what constitutes political life and in asserting that, *qua* expression of view, speech has a right, if a defeasible one, to be permitted, I am not embracing a position of liberal relativism. According to that, censorship is unjustified because any viewpoint is as good as any other. That position is incoherent, since its premise entails that the view that censorship is justified is 'as good as' the view that it is not. Relativism, by denying the role of rational criticism, confrontation with the facts and objective reflection, threatens respect for the value of free thought and discussion. For beliefs are expressed and argued for as true and well-founded; to say 'this is my belief and I have a right to it whatever the truth may be, or whatever objections there may be', is absurd.[10] But if my views are censored, then I cannot but see the suppression of their expression, in the first instance, as a mere manifestation of power – as an indication that you do not like what I am saying and want to stop me. Unlike criticism, in which critics and criticised have to address common issues, and in which there are objective standards of argument, it is the censorious position that partakes of relativism: by insisting that whatever views you believe to be vicious you have a right to suppress, you grant the principle to your opponent, and make what *is* in fact suppressed a function, not of the merits of the case, but of power. This is one reason why Popper's Millian and idealised portrait of the scientific community, with its rights of opposition, and its pursuit of truth by submission to refutation, perhaps merits more respectful attention from socialists than it has gained. The closed society which Popper opposes, after all, is the society where only the 'correct' thought can be spoken, where to have a platform is, of itself, to have one's views endorsed.

If my argument has been framed in terms, embedded in the liberal tradition, of 'rational autonomy', it has also depended on ideas of 'benefits' flowing from freedom: the development of human capacities, openness of communication and growth in knowledge and understanding. Since Mill's attempt, the reconciliation of the 'greatest happiness principle' with notions of quasi-'absolute' rights has been recognised as problematic. I do not claim to have done much more than re-stir the dust which seems to have settled on concerns which the intelligentsia has left to the Activists and their establishment Guardians. But it should be pointed out that my argument depends on claims of 'very general facts' about the way minds work and the role of discourse in that working. It does not depend on a purely

10 See Trevor Pateman's discussion in Pateman 1980.

abstract value of 'autonomy', such that the right to express and examine ideas would be held sacred irrespective of any views as to the 'natural light' which reason sheds and demands. As the opening quotations from Marx and Heine indicate, the arguments for censorship tend to assume a more or less incapable mass under the guidance of a more or less infallible authority. If the world were like that, Plato's republic would be its utopia. In this respect my position differs from the related one of Thomas Scanlon (1977). Scanlon's argument, based on Kant, claims to be *independent* of claims that freedom of speech 'would, in the long run, have more good consequences than bad' (*ibid.*, p. 161) or that 'the truth is more likely to win out if free discussion is allowed' (*ibid.*, p. 165). It seems to me that anyone rejecting such empirical claims had better join the authoritarians. 'Autonomy' and 'rational consent' have value only if the human mind's natural causality is to be more or less reasonable, and only if the equally natural countervailing practice of closure and protection is, in its general tendency, harmful.

But, in so far as the case for freedom of speech is one which depends on 'very general facts' about the role of discourse, and especially in so far as it focuses on the 'harms' of censorship, it must recognise that the grounds offered for censorship, if inadequate, are not thereby spurious. Speech can harm in diverse ways: it can delude, dazzle, cruelly wound or incite to evil action. The possibility of justifiable censorship cannot be ruled out *a priori.* All that a general article of this kind can do is seek to show that, if it may be necessary to 'save the village' through censorship, it cannot but be at the cost of damaging it. In contrast, the open confrontation and criticism of delusions, the debunking of dazzlers, the education of the susceptible and the fortification of the butts of derision are positive modes of struggle that strengthen rather than corrupt the self-correcting powers of society. Such a path is not a secure one, and it is clearly highly vulnerable in isolation from a general shift of the social formation away from its present class-ridden culture, with its consequent poverty of thought and spirit.

2

The account, so far, has been global and abstract. It has talked generally about 'speech' without clarifying the scope of that term. It has treated censorship as the standard way of restricting speech without examining the many conditions of cultural freedom. I now propose to examine in more detail what I take to be constituents of freedom of speech. While this will entail qualifications to some of the general claims above, its principal function will be to locate the struggle for freedom of speech in the context of a wider struggle for social liberation. This is not to say that it is only in such a context that resistance to censorship has value; I have argued that censorship is an evil worth resisting in itself. But it is to say that absence of censorship is not a sufficient condition of freedom of speech.

We can ask: *what sort of speech is compelled or restricted*? John Locke's *Letter concerning toleration* contested the compulsion publicly to avow orthodox religious views to secure civil rights. Despite the obvious state context, Locke's argument reminds us that not only 'political' discourse can be a political right and that restrictions on blasphemy, sexual explicitness and personal insult *are* restrictions on freedom of speech. In the assessment of a society's freedom of speech it is blinkered to ignore speech at all levels, from debate over matters of state to the discussion of a family problem ('Shut up; this is none of your business').[11]

The phrase 'sorts of speech' suggests a genus with more or less clear species. But speech-acts have diverse dimensions and descriptions: 'saying', 'interrupting', 'asking', 'shouting', 'insulting', 'disturbing', 'enlightening', are all words that could apply to *one* act: 'And what were *you* doing while all this was happening under your nose, Mr President?' Clearly, not all the dimensions of a speech-act are defensible under the terms of 'freedom of speech', whose central focus is on the expression of ideas: we are not concerned with defending the right to make as much noise as one likes. Yet, as becomes clear if one thinks, for

[11] Scanlon 1977, p. 155, takes 'generality of interest' and size of audience as 'typical' features of situations where freedom of speech is at issue.

example, of the significance in large public meetings of the right to use the microphone, noise levels can be relevant to questions of freedom of speech.

More generally, we need to be clear about what relevantly counts as 'speech'. If radio and television transmit 'speech', is it not arbitrary in this context not to treat as speech the contents of newspapers, posters and magazines? And are not gestures, assemblies and marches usefully thought of as forms of speech – as ways of making 'statements' – protests, appeals?[12] That such ways entail the more or less exclusive occupation of more or less valuable space in more or less physically disturbing ways does not count against their status as 'statements' – but does render them properly subject to specific constraints. If the expression and communication of ideas is the focal character of 'speech' in relation to its being a central freedom, then it seems to me right to use 'speech' in this quite general sense in this context.

It is well to remember, however, that the chapter in *On liberty* in which Mill addresses this issue is entitled 'Of the liberty of thought and discussion' while Scanlon's paper is on 'Freedom of expression'. There is a danger that the generic term 'speech' might distract from the specific significance, scopes and limitations of media. There is, further, a need to be aware of specific conditions and values of speech narrowly defined (think of lectures, conversations, seminars, public meetings). But an illuminating account of freedom would need to look beyond vocal expression. Now that the 'town-meeting' has been supplanted as the dominant model of 'democracy' by technologically orchestrated election campaigns, it is more than ever necessary to treat newspapers, magazines and leaflets as containing 'speech' alongside television and radio programmes and what is said through telephones and walkie-talkies, without forgetting that you can

[12] I find support for this and later claims in the Home Office's *Review of the Public Order Act, 1936 and Related Legislation* (Cmnd. 7801) HMSO April 1980. Arguing against claims that marches are not 'on a par with' speech, the report goes on: 'those who participate in marches regard them as an important means of expressing their views. Access to the media is not equally available and a ban on all political marches might bear more heavily on the relatively disadvantaged' (p. 11).

answer back through the telephone but not through the television set.[13]

To talk of 'media' is to talk, not only of *ways* of 'speaking', but of the scope and power of *communication*. Media are 'means', of communicating and of being communicated with.

Suppose you were given freedom to 'say what you like' but only in the wilderness where few could be expected to hear. Freedom of speech is something which *speakers* enjoy or lack. This truism is important because it makes it harder to think that what is wrong with interference with speech is just that it 'robs' potential receivers of information to store or act on. Exclusive focus on audiences, and on rights of information, approached by Mill and Scanlon with their emphasis on the withholding from us of others' possibly relevant opinions, leads to an inadequate view.[14] I could be denied freedom of speech though you get an accurate account of what I would have said, or though what I would have said is common knowledge. But, on the other hand, to ignore reception entails a truncating abstraction of the speech act, a failure to see that speech is fundamentally communication and that audiences are constitutive of speech situations. It would be absurd to think that only receivers' rights were violated by the blocking of communication; every totalitarian society permits its members to mutter in the solitude of their toilets. Censorship aims to block communication and the enforced absence of an audience 'gags' the speaker as well as 'robbing' those who might hear. Does that mean that to have freedom of speech you must actually get a hearing? That would entail, not only that means of access to (chosen?) audiences would have to be available, but that they actually listened to me. A (conceptually) impossible burden would thereby be placed on time, space, resources and powers of attention as everyone demanded rapt attention of each other. Freedom of speech cannot entail compulsion to listen; indeed, it is incompatible with it, since, while I am forced to listen, I am incapacitated from speaking. Audiences and poten-

[13] For a discussion of these matters, Robin Murray, Tom Wengraf and Stephen Hymer's *The political economy of communications* (Spokesman Pamphlet no. 5., Nottingham, 1970) is excellent.

[14] See Dworkin's editorial criticism of Scanlon in Scanlon 1977, p. 15.

tial audiences have rights, a further indication of the need to look at freedom in speech situations.

Does that mean on the other hand that, as is claimed by the juridically minded, freedom of speech is in no way threatened by the voluntary inattention – 'ignoring', 'refusal to listen' – of others? *Suppose everybody walked out of the room every time unpopular views began to be expressed* (to point up the agony, let the reader suppose him or herself to be speaking). They do not heckle, or chant or threaten to beat up the speaker; 'they do not interfere in any way'. Now, while these people have not voted that you cannot speak, have not prevented you from speaking and have not prevented anyone else from hearing, it is clear that such a practice is incompatible with the activity of rational debate or discussion and that a way of life in which people normally refused to listen to views opposed to their own would not be an open society or one in which freedom of speech could flourish. It would appear that freedom of speech, then, requires a culture in which minds are critically open. It is evident that such a cultural desideratum cannot be guaranteed by a legal constitution, but requires embodiment in social traditions and practices and especially in forms of education. It is an important theme of the feminist movement that 'hearing' and 'ignoring' are socially structured political powers, that males' 'choosing not to listen' is a function of being in a position not to *have* to listen; in a position 'to afford' not to care what women say.

To talk about this 'informal' cultural dimension is to highlight the substantial judgements that are inextricable from judgements about freedom of speech. If people walk out on opposed views rather than rebutting them, they probably exhibit little feeling for speech's freedom. Yet walking out on a speech can itself be a protesting statement of this very value – 'This hearing is a travesty'; 'If you will not allow discussion, this meeting is not worth attending'. Generally, 'editing' and procedural structure are necessary conditions of discourse. They involve countless, often spontaneous, often contestable judgements: 'You are filibustering', 'You are speaking out of turn', 'You are not addressing the point', 'You are repeating what has been said', 'You are hogging the discussion', 'You have not answered the question'. All these claims, typical of the practice of communication, could justify restricting speeches without being an interference with freedom of speech.[15] Absolutists, who say either that all speech must be heard or, at the other extreme, that no one is ever obliged to give a hearing to anything, ignore the necessarily substantial and particular judgements that are at issue in deciding whether freedom of speech has been denied or violated.[16] The editor who suppresses 'that sort of view' from the town newspaper is different from the one who refuses to publish a full-page account of a speech at the neighbourhood card tournament. Both differ from the editors of a libertarian paper who refuse space to authoritarian views well-aired elsewhere. Not that such editorial prerogatives do not tend to be exploited in the direction of closure sketched in the last paragraph, as editors protect the 'fugitive and cloistered virtue' which Milton and Mill saw to be inimical to freedom.

Suppose you could say what you liked but that few would hear you unless you bought time on the media or had to be vetted by those owning the media. If access to audiences is part of full freedom of speech, questions of means of access and of their control and distribution come to the fore. Speech-acts are often 'broadcasts' in our society. 'From 1815, newspapers had to carry a fourpenny stamp, a "tax on knowledge", which effectively and explicitly priced newspapers out of the pockets of the poor' (Hollis 1970, preface). Mill recognised the illiberally 'prohibitive' character of such legislation (Mill 1962, p. 233), though *On liberty* failed to consider the implications of monopolies of wealth for powers of speech. The printed word opened up lines of communication for different social forces. At the same time, because, unlike air and breath, paper and printing are costly and because literacy needed to be specially taught, it opened up ways of controlling those lines.

Speech in the narrow sense makes possible reciprocal communication between people given that they can speak the language. Explicit rules of silence ('unless you are spoken to'), monopolies of codes and sub-codes prevent some from doing what they facilitate others in doing. 'Powers of speech' are differentially acquired in the context of everyday learning, both

[15] Compare Meiklejohn 1948.
[16] See reference above to the Home Office Report.

in respect of rhetoric and vocabulary.[17] If societies have microphones, radios, televisions, telephones, recording equipment, walkie-talkies and meeting halls, it is obvious that questions of freedom of speech – of who is prevented from speaking – cannot be considered in isolation from questions of reasonable distribution. (It is in this light that mass heckling can be seen as 'access-redistribution'. Though it can pass into bullying suppression, heckling is often a measure of the indomitability of those disenfranchised from full political participation.) Property rights in printing and broadcasting are rights to control speech. An open, 'literate' society would require a 'free press' structured by other than capitalist or central state criteria. Otherwise, voices of opposition are threatened with being submerged by the orchestrated thoughts of the monopolies. Explicit censorship and restrictive licensing are only two ways of controlling speech – I don't stop you from talking if I turn up my loud-hailer until your voice cannot be heard.

In this regard, the 'sensible' view of the Annan *Report on the future of broadcasting* is lame:

> It does not follow that, because by a flick of a switch you can cut me off and stop listening, I have a right of access to the medium, since there is a limited amount of time and air space. To declare that every citizen, or even any organised group, has a right of access to a frequency is to imply that the Government, or a Broadcasting Authority, has an obligation to provide air-time. But governments cannot afford, or are unable, to give some people what they call their rights . . . Broadcasting is not a mass conversation. Broadcasting is in fact a form of publishing: not a dialogue or the equivalent of a Witenagemot.[18]

The Committee appears to move from the true and uncontentious point that access is limited to the dubious claim that 'rights of access' are a bogus demand. But then, what would confer legitimate rights of access to ITV or Rupert Murdoch's spiritual hit-squad? Wisdom? Money? It is true that the development of fair freedom of communication entails the allocation of scarce resources, which thereby places this freedom in competition with other goods (as well as bads) and entails 'balancing'. But that is

[17] See Bernstein 1965, pp. 145–66. See also Labov 1977.

[18] *Report of the committee on the future of broadcasting* (Cmnd. 6573) HMSO, 1977, para 3.14.

only to say that democratic freedom has costs, as the police protection of National Front marches in any case indicates.

Suppose you were allowed to say what you liked, but denied access to information on which to ground what you say. It is a conceptual truth that speech aims at an audience; but if speech aims to communicate it also aims to communicate *something*. You have something to say when you have something to say that is, or seems to be, 'reasonable'. This is a precondition of what you say being worth hearing. If people do not think that what you have to say has any connection with reality they do not 'take you seriously'. This gives reason for regarding the withholding of information to *speakers* as an attack on freedom of speech, at least in so far as speech-acts purport to be acts of 'informing' or 'telling the truth'. A society in which Official Secrets Acts and company laws of property in information leave much room for semi-ignorant, scotchable and servile rumour, but in which the dominant institutions hold a relative monopoly of 'grounds for assertion' (hence scope for unchecked deceit and propaganda) is a society in which speech is not free.

If this is right, then 'freedom of information', of a kind deemed constitutional in the United States, but subversive in the United Kingdom, is at least a precondition of genuine freedom of speech. This entails some paradoxes: it means, for example that some people's speech must be unfree, since they *must* divulge information, and it entails some deep problems; for example problems over rights of privacy. I can do nothing but advertise these problems here with the comment that their use in this country to frighten off the pursuit of reasonable freedom of information is a good reason for thinking the pursuit important.

Suppose you can talk freely and informedly but that your discussion plays no role in the processes by which the powers-that-be make decisions. Where speech is engaged in under the description 'making a suggestion' but where the hearer's mind is made up, an 'unhappiness', in Austin's infelicitous phrase, occurs. Some such unhappinesses, of course, are inevitable. But do structurally ignored groups have freedom of speech in the sort of 'tolerantly despotic' situation envisaged above? John Rawls would probably say that they do but that their freedom of speech has little 'worth' in the absence of broader democratic freedoms (Rawls 1972, p. 204). This view might be defended by contrasting structurally impotent speech with a pseudo-election where people are allowed to state their preferences, but where this does not determine the outcome: such people lack the right to *vote*. Voting, it could be argued, is conceptually closer to being counted than is talking to being taken notice of. But an indefinite connection may still be a necessary one, and this is reflected in the naturalness of saying that one was not 'listened to' in such circumstances. Certainly, the sorts of speech-act that constitute political discourse: advocating, advising, defending, complaining, pleading, petitioning, persuading, planning, presuppose potential practical uptake. To the extent that the basic description of a speech-act requires this potential, its absence nullifies freedom to engage in it. This does not establish that there is *no* freedom of speech, because the powerless can still discuss, analyse, theorise, grumble and joke – real, if stunted, liberties.

My account of freedom of speech, then, entails that it could be part of a political 'constitution', not just as a juridical right to utter and hear certain words, but as a network of powers exercised and maintained in a free and democratic community.[19] Freedom of speech requires a radical transformation of much of the institutional structure of societies such as Britain's: from their central state institution to the organisation of the press, industry and education. This assertion does not flow from a Marcusian dismissal of the liberties that exist in contemporary society. It is not the case that the majority are culturally caged parrots in the keeping of totalitarian masters. Nonetheless, since the advent of bourgeois liberalism it has been clear that the 'sound minds and good wills' which the liberals took to be given by man's status as a rational being need to be cultivated and that the natural light of reason can be starved of fuel and blocked by smog. Libertarian democracy does entail risks; in the absence of religious faith in the popular mind it must be recognised that democratic argument can be sophistical and that democratic conclusions can be mistaken. But democratic values depend on trust in the give and take of open argument, and on the educative

[19] Compare Anderson 1941.

function of engaging in it; just as much as they depend on mistrust of those who would protect us from those risks by supplanting open conflict of ideas with the activities of committees for the safety of the public mind.[20]

REFERENCES

Anderson, J. 1941. Art and morality. *Australasian Journal of Psychology and Philosophy*, 19, pp. 241–66.

Bernstein, B. 1965. A socio-linguistic approach to social learning. In *Penguin survey of the social sciences*, ed. J. Gould, pp. 145–66. Harmondsworth, Penguin.

Clor, H. M. 1969. *Obscenity and public morality*. Chicago University Press.

Easton, L. and Guddat, K. 1967. *Writings of the young Marx on philosophy and society*. New York, Anchor.

Fried, C. 1978. *Right and wrong*. Cambridge, Mass., Harvard University Press.

Heine, H. 1975. *Selections*. London, Everyman.

Hollis, P. 1970. *The pauper press*. London, Oxford University Press.

Labov, W. 1977. *Language and the inner city*. Oxford University Press.

Locke, J. 1963. *A letter concerning toleration*. The Hague, Martinus Nijhoff.

MacDonald, I. A. 1977. *Race relations – the new law*. London, Butterworth.

Marcuse, H., Wolff, R. P. and Moore, B. 1965. *A critique of pure tolerance*. Boston, Harper and Row.

Meiklejohn, A. 1948. *Political freedom*. New York, Harper and Bros.

Mill, J. S. 1962. *On liberty*, ed. M. Warnock. London, Fontana.

Murray, R., Wengraf, T. and Hymer, S. 1970. *The political economy of communications*. Nottingham, Spokesman Pamphlet no. 5.

Pateman, T. 1980. *Language, truth and politics*. Lewes, Jean Stroud.

Popper, K. R. 1962. *The open society and its enemies*, vol. I. London, Routledge and Kegan Paul.

Rawls, J. 1972. *A theory of justice*. London, Oxford University Press.

Scanlon, T. 1977. A theory of freedom of expression. In *The philosophy of law*, ed. R. Dworkin, pp. 153–71. Oxford University Press.

Skillen, A. 1980. How to say things with walls. *Philosophy*, 55, pp. 509–23.

[20] Many discussions have helped in the development of this article. I would especially like to thank Keith Graham and Richard Norman and Ross Poole for their criticism of a previous draft.